By the same author
The Land-Rover
The Mighty-MGs

THE RANGE ROVER / LAND-ROVER

GRAHAM ROBSON

DAVID & CHARLES
Newton Abbot   London   North Pomfret (Vt)

British Library Cataloguing in Publication Data

Robson, Graham
    The Range Rover/Land-Rover – 2nd ed.
    1. Land-Rover truck – History
    2. Range Rover truck – History
    I. Title
    629.2′222   TL230.5.L36

    ISBN 0–7153–8786–3

Printed in Great Britain
by Redwood Burn Limited, Trowbridge, Wiltshire
for David & Charles Publishers plc
Brunel House   Newton Abbot   Devon

Published in the United States of America
by David & Charles Inc
North Pomfret   Vermont 05053   USA

Contents

Introduction

'A touch of genius'? Why not? There is plenty of evidence to support this. No machine could continue to sell in such huge numbers for more than thirty years unless it was rather special. No ordinary machine would attract so many imitators. And if it was so easy to match the Land-Rover's abilities, why have so many competitors failed to make the grade?

You cannot call a machine which has sold by the million a phenomenon—not any more. You cannot explain its long-running success in terms of advanced technology. Not now, anyway, though when conceived in 1947 it was a thoroughly modern concept. Quite simply, a Land-Rover is, and always has been, the right product for the job. You can measure that by the way its name is now used to describe all such machines. Like Hoover, Mini and Biro, the original has become the generic name for the type.

Yet when Spencer and Maurice Wilks invented the Land-Rover they had no idea what sort of a phenomenon they were launching. To them, at the time, it was merely a useful stopgap to fill up the new Solihull factory when private car production was lagging behind. By the early 1950s, however, when Land-Rovers were already outselling Rover private cars, there was no doubt that it had become a permanent (and very profitable) fixture.

Not even the turbulent take-over years, and the first precarious build-up of British Leyland, could disturb the Land-Rover. Other marques, faced with possible rationalisation, trembled for their very existence. The Land-Rover merely looked forward to greater and greater success. Within two years, indeed, it had been joined by the plushy and prestigious Range Rover.

Since 1968 British Leyland has been battered by all manner of disasters, and is now a nationalised concern. Through all this, Rover's four-wheel drive machines have sailed serenely on. Demand is enormous, and growing, and the waiting lists show no sign of disappearing. The final seal of approval came in 1978 when they were given their own autonomous company, Land-Rover Limited, which is now the 'landlord' at Solihull and is one of the three branches of the Jaguar-Rover-Triumph division, has its own complete management team, and is now forging ahead with a vast expansion programme.

Three years ago David & Charles Limited published my first book about these splendid machines to celebrate the building of the millionth Land-Rover, which could do no more than summarise the success story and mention the later developments. I am grateful to them for giving me the opportunity to produce a new volume, which concentrates more on the up-market Range Rover, and other Land-Rover products which have matured in the meantime.

Talks with Land-Rover Limited management have convinced me that there will be Land-Rovers on the market for many years to come. That, and the details of future expansion at Solihull which I have been shown, means that the story is by no means complete. I am delighted!

Graham Robson
May 1979

Introduction to Revised Edition

In the six years since this book was originally published, the Land-Rover range has been completely modernised, and the Range Rover is more versatile than ever before. A great deal has been done to keep Solihull's 4 x 4s up-to-date, and continued production into the 1990s is already assured.

This, then, is the story so far. Perhaps I ought to leave space for even more, in the years to come!

Graham Robson
June 1985

1 Inspiration —
the Land-Rover is Born

The Land-Rover is now world famous, and has been called the most versatile vehicle in the business. Well over a million have now been delivered, and after thirty years of production the demand is higher than ever. Land-Rovers are now such an integral part of the industrial and agricultural scene that it is impossible to visualise a world without them. Yet, for all that, the Rover company never looked on their Land-Rover as a long-term project when it was being designed in 1947. Indeed, if they could have looked into their future, at that moment, they might have found the vision incredible.

It is a fact that the Land-Rover was vital to Rover's survival in the 1940s. We must make no mistake about this. Before the Land-Rover went on sale, Rover were building too many of the wrong type of cars. Because of the Land-Rover's success, Rover rapidly changed, and expanded rapidly. It was the machine which upset Rover's cosy middle-class image, upset their expectations, and placed them firmly in the British big league. Although the Land-Rover was developed in a hurry as a short-term stopgap, it has lived on triumphantly to become the stopgap which broke all records.

The Land-Rover's birth was due to a depressing sequence of events in post-war Britain. Commercially it came about because of a nearly empty factory, because of a drastic shortage of sheet steel, and because of the government's insistence on production for export. Emotionally, it came about because of the shortcomings of some ex-military machinery, and to satisfy the needs of a land-owner in Anglesey, North Wales, in 1947.

To set the scene, I must summarise the Rover company's more recent history. The company was founded in Coventry, and had been building cars since 1904. After production of pedal cycles and motor cycles had ceased in the 1920s, car production was expanded rapidly—too rapidly, as it happens, for the sales that could be achieved, and for the quality that could be maintained. After 1929 the company was rescued from impending financial collapse by Spencer Wilks, who had previously been Joint Managing Director of the Hillman concern, which was also in Coventry.

Spencer Wilks, soon joined at Rover by his younger brother Maurice (who was a trained design engineer), spent the 1930s changing Rover's image, and charting its long-term future. His new policy can be summarised as 'Quality First', and he limited car production to concentrate on building elegant middle-price machines. By 1936 he had gained so much rsepect for the dramatic improvement made to Rover that the company was invited to join in the Air Ministry's 'shadow factory' scheme. It was this which, indirectly and in a way not to be foreseen at the time, led to Rover's 1947 crisis.

The 'shadow factories' were erected and paid for by the British government, in order to make aeroplane engines. Each particular factory was to be staffed and operated on a fee-paying basis by a company in the motor industry. The first factory allocated to Rover

Maurice Wilks (hand on drawing board), on whose farm in North Wales the germ of the Land-Rover project developed, talks technicalities with Robert Boyle, his chief designer

on this basis was at Acocks Green—between the main built-up area of Birmingham and the pleasant residential town of Solihull—and it was in production by the end of 1937. The second, a much larger affair, was located on the northern outskirts of Solihull; building work began in 1939, and the first components were machined there in 1940.

After World War II began in September 1939, Rover concentrated all their efforts on production of aeroplane engines, and airframes, together with many other items of military equipment. Eventually they were rewarded with important development contracts concerning the secret new gas-turbine engines, and in 1943 these were exchanged (with Rolls-Royce Ltd) for rights to build Rolls-Royce vee-12 Meteor tank engines. Enemy action had little effect on Rover's activities, except for two severe bombing raids on the Helen Street, Coventry factory in 1940 and 1941, which resulted in considerable damage, only repaired at the time on a temporary basis.

Even before war had threatened, Spencer Wilks had presented his medium-term expansion plans to the other directors. In 1938 Rover had built 10,516 cars, and Wilks recommended that a steady but evolutionary increase in production should be carried out, without the cars being changed in any radical way likely to unsettle the clientele. In 1944, however, the company's future looked less stable, and several vitally important decisions would have to be taken.

One concerned the products to be made, and the other concerned where they were to be built. By the end of the 1930s the Helen Street plant was bursting at the seams, and after the war it was with great relief that Spencer Wilks heard that Rover would be given first refusal in regard to the 'shadow factories' in Acocks Green and Solihull.

There and then it was decided that Acocks Green should carry on, even in peacetime, building the Meteor tank engines (for which there was an assured future), while the vast Solihull works should become the centre of private car production. Helen Street would be sold as it stood, and the company's headquarters would therefore move out of Coventry for the first time in nearly seventy years.

At this time there were great joys *and* awful frustrations. Like others in the British motor industry, Rover applied for permission to start civilian car production at the end of 1944, were refused at first, but were later given the go-ahead—on the basis of a steel allocation sufficient to build a mere 1,100 cars. Nevertheless, Spencer Wilks presented his new plan for the company's future, in which he envisaged immediate production of 15,000 cars a year of the pre-war 'P2' type, along with another 5,000 cars a year of an entirely new design, one to be rated at only 6hp (British RAC rating).

All this was on the assumption that production could get under way rapidly, that raw material supplies would be assured, and that a return to peacetime conditions would be swift. It was a vain hope. On the one hand, and within weeks of the end of the war in the summer of 1945, most of the company's military contracts were rapidly terminated, and the jigs and fixtures cleared away. On the other hand, the government let it be known that supplies of every type of material, but most particularly of sheet steel for body pressings, would be severely rationed. A company which would not, or could not, export the major portion of its output, would not find favour.

Rover were in a real quandary. Not only had they never exported cars in any quantity, but they had never (in more than 40 years) built cars with left-hand drive. Nor were they convinced that the classic and elegant P2 models would sell well in export territories. The new small car—the 'M' Type—was designed with two objects in mind, one as a car to be more universally saleable, and the other to use aluminium alloy pressings for body panels *and* box-section chassis members, to get round the sheet steel shortage.

By the beginning of 1947, however, work on the little 'M' Type was shelved, as it was thought that in fact it lacked export potential. This, compounded with the potential high cost of tooling up for a new structure and a new engine, changes in car taxation laws in Britain (a flat-rate annual tax was being introduced), and government pressure on all car firms to adopt a 'one model' production policy, sealed its fate.

Rover now had a very serious problem. Although P2 production had been transferred smoothly enough from Coventry to Solihull, the cars were still not even being built at 1939 rates. Solihull was big— very big—and in financial terms was simply eating its head off without producing enough to keep the accountants happy. Quite simply, if work could not be found to fill the empty spaces at Solihull—and found very quickly—Rover could be in serious financial trouble.

By this time, Rover had settled on their plan for post-war private car production, and the designs had been agreed. The existing P2 types, which were still only being built at the rate of about 4,000 cars a year, would be phased out by the end of 1947, and would be replaced by the interim P3 models, which would feature a brand new engine having overhead inlet and side exhaust valves, a unit which had been under development since the late 1930s. After a further two years or so, P3 was to be replaced by P4, which was all new apart from the engine, and for which a £250,000 investment in body shell tooling had already been approved.

To keep the Solihull factory and its workforce busy, and to help Rover pay its way until the P4 was properly in quantity production, the Wilks brothers therefore cast around for some sort of stopgap, which could be any vehicle, they reasoned, which would sell well and could be put into production quickly, and which would require the absolute minimum of capital investment. The company was already in enough potential financial trouble without committing its reserves to more tooling, which would in any case take ages to be delivered.

After all manner of possibilities had been discussed and rejected, the brothers gradually began to warm to the idea of building some sort of agricultural vehicle or machine. Although Rover had no tradition, nor any experience, in this field, it was quite clear that there was a huge pent-up world-wide demand for mechanised agricultural appliances. It was not that the ravages of war had extended to this category of machine, causing an artificial shortage, but that farmers all over the world were raising their standards. Tractor tycoon Harry Ferguson, with his new and very effective designs, was already beginning to tap the same market. Much of the world was now ready, it seemed, to swap horses and nose bags for engines and petrol cans.

In the first months of 1947 the brothers, while convinced of the type of machine they should produce, were not agreed as to its precise nature, and for a time they agreed to carry out separate studies. It is now well known that it was Maurice Wilks, and his estate in North Wales, which provided the vital spark. Maurice had had the house and farmland on the island of Anglesey for some years; the 250 acres included normal farmland, woods, sand dunes, and a share of the coastline. He could not spend much time there, particularly during and immediately after the war, but he liked to get his hands well and truly dirty when he snatched a weekend in the country. Maurice Wilks was by no means a 'gentleman farmer'.

His basic problem on this estate was that he needed a machine to do everything for him; he needed power to pull a plough, to haul logs, to drive stationary machines, and something that would keep going on any surface, up or down the steepest of gradients, in and out of water. This vehicle, he reasoned, would have to be a four-wheel drive or cross-country machine. First of all he had bought an ex-WD half-track

Ford truck, which had Ford's powerful 3.6-litre V8 engine, but this was bulky, unwieldy, not at all economical, and very limited in road use.

He therefore replaced the old Ford truck with another military vehicle, one of the ubiquitous Willys Jeeps which the American forces had introduced to Britain in 1942. Jeeps were in plentiful supply; they were cheap and they were reliable. As a working vehicle it was better than the truck, if not ideal, but it rankled the patriotic Wilks that he needed to use imported machinery to do his work.

Although the Jeep was doing a good job, it was beginning to look battered by the time Spencer Wilks visited his brother to talk over the Solihull problem; the story goes that the elder brother then asked Maurice what he proposed to do when the Jeep finally fell apart? 'Buy another one,' said Maurice. 'There isn't *anything* else I can buy.'

Quite suddenly, it seems, this crystallised their thinking. If Maurice Wilks, with a typical cross-section of requirements from his farm machinery, could think of no answer to his problem, perhaps Rover should set about designing one? This, then, was to be Rover's gap-plugger, and the final decision was taken after another long thrash in the willing Jeep around the Anglesey estate.

Immediately after that momentous weekend in the country, Maurice Wilks came back to the Solihull offices on the Monday morning and initiated the project. He had no other guidance from the sales departments, and product planning as we know it today simply did not exist. It was even Maurice Wilks who christened the new project—Land-Rover

Worm's-eye view of the very first Land-Rover prototype chassis, complete with Jeep chassis (modified) and the familiar four-wheel drive layout. The chassis was stiffened up considerably before production began

—at the very beginning of the project. He was already convinced that he had found an ideal stopgap.

He was quite wrong about the stopgap, but triumphantly right about everything else. In the beginning, it was designer Gordon Bashford who was instructed to draw up the original layout, on no more specific brief than that the new vehicle should be 'like a Jeep', and that it should use as many existing Rover parts as possible. It should also be as simple as possible—brutally simple, in fact—so that capital expenditure for tooling should be as little as possible.

Bashford has this to say about the project, as it was introduced to him in the spring of 1947:

It was really very much like the Jeep at first. It is no coincidence that the wheelbase and the basic dimensions were all repeated in the Land-Rover, as I based my original package around the Jeep. In the very first vehicle we used a lot of Jeep material, and almost automatically that meant we could use the same important dimensions.

The machine I laid out at first had no doors (these were going to be optional extras!), no trim, no hood as such—and it even had a central driving position and steering wheel, with chain drive to a steering box on the appropriate side of the scuttle!

The body, such as it was, would be made out of aluminium. That was partly because of the sheet metal shortage, and partly to give the best possible corrosion protection. It helped a lot when we came to forming the panels, because aluminium alloy is that much easier to work.

The definitive Land-Rover chassis layout, Series I variety. Note that this chassis has a bolt-on, not an integral, front bumper. Almost every component has been changed since then, but the Land-Rover basic layout remains the same

The unique centre-seat Land-Rover prototype of 1947, which unfortunately does not survive, having been converted to a conventional layout later in the year. The body 'style' was vastly different from that eventually put on sale

The main problem was not one of engineering, but of time. In this case there simply was not time to indulge in the usual ultra-cautious Rover design and development time-scales. Even in the 1930s, when it was much easier to get prototype items built very speedily, it was quite usual for a car to stagger haltingly into production a good two years after the go-ahead had taken place. Because of the burning urgency of the entire project, the Land-Rover was pushed through at breakneck speed. Work began in the spring of 1947—probably in April, though no one is now sure of this—the first prototype was complete by the end of the summer, and the Land-Rover was announced at the end of April 1948, with deliveries beginning during the summer.

In fact the company was not ready to start production when the Land-Rover was announced, but this premature release was done so that any important initial reactions could be included in changes made to the machine at the last minute. As it happens the Land-Rover's reception was little short of rapturous, and the only important change was to standardise much of the all-weather equipment which was originally intended to be extra.

The key to the speed at which the project took shape, indeed the key to the whole Land-Rover project, was the Jeep. In the beginning the Rover designers, with no experience of their own, looked closely at the Jeep, copied where appropriate, and improved in many ways. It meant that there were no major mistakes in the concept, which made development and finalisation that much easier.

There is no question of sharp practice here, nor of any Jeep trade marks or especially any patents being infringed. Maurice Wilks admired his own much-used Jeep, and admired what it could do for his farm. He was certainly not averse to learning from its good features, and discarding its bad ones. There is nothing new in this. All car makers did it then, and still do it today.

Maurice Wilks' brief to his design team was simple and straight-forward, as Land-Rover Limited's technical director, Tom Barton, recalls:

Maurice Wilks wanted us to design a vehicle very like the Jeep, but it had to be even more useful to a farmer. That was the point—it was to be a proper farm machine, not just another Jeep. He wanted it to be much more versatile, much more use as a power source. He wanted it to be able to drive things, to have power take-offs *everywhere*, and to have all sorts of bolt-on accessories, and to be used instead of a tractor at times. It had to be able to do everything!

I was one of five section leaders in the design drawing office, and each of us was given the job of designing part of the new device—the Land-Rover. We had a very broad brief, nothing detailed, except that we were asked to make a vehicle similar to the Jeep. My first job was to graft a new transfer box on the back of an existing car gearbox, the P3 box.

We thought about accessories straight away. I also had to think about power take-offs and things—so that the Land-Rover could be useful to the farmer in every way.

Gordon Bashford once told me that one of his first tasks was to go off to a vast Army surplus dump in the Cotswolds to buy two more Jeeps (to add to Maurice Wilks' own example, which had found its way back to the factory from North Wales). Both were immediately stripped down to their component parts, some for unabashed study by the designers, and some actually to be used to help build the first Land-Rover prototype, which was very definitely a half-breed. The original Land-Rover, for instance, was built up around a renovated Jeep chassis frame, as this saved a great deal of time.

So the Land-Rover, even today, owes something to the Jeep in its concept, but how closely related were the two machines at first? In general concept, certainly, the two designs were very similar. This, of course, says much for the innovative layout of the original Jeep, which was—and still is—a great success. That said, I must point out that there is really only one logical way of laying out the design of any four-wheel drive machine having a front engine and one gearbox. In other words, both designs had separate box-section chassis frames, front-mounted engines, gearboxes in unit with their engine, transfer gearing behind that box, and propeller shafts running forward and back to live front and rear axles. Both had half-elliptic road springs and telescopic dampers.

In detail, however, there were obvious and important differences:

Comparison of 1947 Land-Rover and 1939–45 Jeep

	Land-Rover	Jeep
Wheelbase (in)	80	80
Length (in)	132	133
Width (in)	60	62
Wheel track (in)	50	48
Engine	4-cyl, 1,595cc, ioev, 69.5 × 105mm, 55bhp (gross), 50bhp (net), at 4,000rpm	4-cyl, 2,199cc, sv, 79.4 × 111.1mm, 60bhp (gross) at 3,600rpm
Transmission	4-speed gearbox, ratios 1.00, 1.49, 2.04, 2.99:1; transfer gear; low range, 2.52 step-down	3-speed gearbox, ratios 1.00, 1.56, 2.665:1; transfer gear; low range, 1.97 step-down
Axle ratios	4.88:1	4.88:1
Tyre size	6.00–16in	6.00–16in
Front/rear suspensions	Live axle, half-elliptic leaf springs, telescopic dampers	Live axle, half-elliptic leaf springs, telescopic dampers
Unladen weight	2,520lb	2,315lb
Payload	Not quoted at announcement	'¼ ton', often exceeded, 800lb normal maximum

ioev = overhead inlet valve, side exhaust valve; sv = side valves

Original Series I Land-Rover driving compartment, with separate instrument pod and high back seats

Gordon Bashford has already explained why the wheelbase dimensions were the same, but the axle ratios were the same by coincidence, purely because Rover already had a 4.88 ratio (as used in the Rover 12) which was considered ideal for the purpose. The tyre size, again, was a function of the all-weather treads which were available (and suitable for the heavy duty job intended), and because of the minimum ground clearance required of the vehicle. The Land-Rover's front axle was based on the P3 axle itself (it would have been far too costly and lengthy a business to design and tool up for new axles at each end of the Land-Rover—as it was, a new front axle tube and steerable front hubs were needed), and the suspension layout was a combination of normal usage and what was considered ideal for the job.

The two engines, naturally, were entirely different. That in the Jeep was its own design, big, lazy and side valve, while the Land-Rover's engine was a version of the new P3 Rover passenger car unit. The biggest basic difference, in spite of superficial similarities, was in the transmission. The Willys Jeep had only three forward speeds, with synchromesh on top and second gears, while the Land-Rover had a modified four-speed P3 gearbox, also with synchromesh on the upper two gears. Both vehicles offered a heavy duty low-range set of ratios, the Jeep having a 1.97 step-down and the Land-Rover an even more useful 2.52 step-down.

Where the Land-Rover really scored, however, was in its versatility. The Jeep, even though it was as agile as a mountain goat, was little more than a personnel carrier which could (and often did) tow light trailers or military pieces. The Land-Rover, however, had provision for power take-off points and other fittings designed into it. The original *Autocar* cutaway drawing of April 1948, for instance, showed a propeller shaft from the tail of the gearbox to the back of the chassis already installed, with a power take-off and belt-drive drum bolted on to the chassis frame; the shaft, it was to be said, was to be standard even though the power take-off was to be extra. (It was not a feature which was standardised on production machines.)

There was also provision for a centre power take-off, useful for driving compressors, generators and other portable equipment, and for a front-mounted capstan winch useful for anything from de-ditching other vehicles to grubbing up trees and bushes.

The body, too, was built up in three pieces, with panels of the light-alloy Birmabright material, and each part could be removed, separately from the other parts, in 15 minutes. The Land-Rover, in a way, was as near to being a grown man's Meccano set as anything yet designed.

The first prototype of all, in fact, was not at all like the Land-Rover just described. In the rush to get a vehicle built, merely to prove that Rover's own engineers had done an adequate job, the original device (which unfortunately no longer exists) was less completely developed. Not only was a Jeep frame used, but an older and completely different engine was fitted.

In 1947, of course, the new P3 range of passenger cars was still being developed, had not been announced to the public, and all its components were in short supply. Engines, in particular, could not immediately be spared, so the very first Land-Rover prototype was given the obsolescent 1,389cc Rover 10 engine instead.

If this engine had been used as anything other than a one-off measure to get a prototype on the road, it would have been a very strange decision. On technical grounds it could only have been justified if the Land-Rover had been very light—far lighter, in fact, than it turned out to be. The Jeep's engine, admittedly in side-valve form, had a 2.2-litre capacity, produced 60bhp and a lot of lusty torque. The 1,389cc Rover 10 unit (with a conventional overhead valve cylinder head, and bore and stroke of 66.5 × 100mm) had been introduced as long ago as 1933. It was the first new engine design brought into production as part of the Spencer Wilks 'Quality First' drive, and even in its 1947 form it was good for less than 40bhp.

There was an alternative version of this engine—the 69 × 100mm, 1,496cc Rover 12 engine—which was also in production, but neither unit was scheduled to find a home in the P3 cars for 1948. For the P3 there was an entirely new design, having overhead inlet and side exhaust valves, a cylinder head/block joint face not at right angles to the cylinder bore centres, and with dimensions of 69.5 × 105mm. In the late 1930s, when design had begun, it was originally a conversion of the existing '100mm engine', but with time it had become entirely special, and not a trace of the old design remained.

Although Gordon Bashford had completed the original sketches for the Land-Rover, the five section leaders then had to complete the detail work, and they all had to take note of Maurice Wilks' directive, that the absolute minimum of new tooling, and an absolute minimum of new parts, should be used. It is to all their credit that the Land-Rover never looked like a 'kit car', nor did any important 'carry-over' component prove unsuitable for the job.

The body proposed for the original vehicle was skimpy in the extreme, and was to be built almost entirely of aluminium alloy, so there were quite literally no press tools needed. Most panels, in any case, were almost entirely flat—only the bonnet and the front wings having any noticeable form, and even these panels could be produced by simple forming operations.

The most important new item, which could have involved considerable investment, was the chassis frame, but even here Rover engineers found their own solution. In more normal times—and certainly if the frame was being tooled up for production today—the side-members and cross-members would have been assembled from deep-drawn steel channel section, delicately shaped at points of minimum and maximum stress, the whole thing being jig-built and welded on complex fixtures. In the case of the 1947 Land-Rover there was no time for this, nor the money to be spent.

It was Gordon Bashford and Olaf Poppe (in charge of production engineering at Rover) who devised a very simple solution—one which persists on all short-wheelbase Land-Rovers built to this day. Their proposal was to build up box-section members from four long strips of sheet steel, and to weld the edges together in long seams!

It was an astonishingly simple proposal, which looked incongruous then, and looks even more primitive today, but it works. For each long side-member there are four plates. The side sheets are flat, but curved in profile where they sweep up over the axles to give bump clearance, whereas the top and bottom sheets are absolutely straight and flat. These are tacked together in rudimentary jigs at first, then continuously welded in another low-cost fixture. That fixture has been in use for more than 30 years.

It sounds very simple, and looks it, but the quantity-production problems were severe. I should emphasise at this point that the Jeep had conventional box-section members, produced on heavy presses. Gordon Bashford gives most of the credit to Poppe:

The original 'four-plate' concept came from Olaf Poppe. So we made up several straight sections from plates, tried out the welding process on each edge, added various cross-members so that we had crude 'ladder' frames, and tried them for twisting and bending strength. This came immediately after Maurice Wilks had asked me to lay out the original package for a very simple vehicle. It was to be a 'work-horse', and very very basic.

As far as I know this method had never been done before by anyone. Anyway, box sections were still quite new to Rover—all the pre-war chassis had been open channel-section frames.

But it was not quite as straightforward as it might have been:

After the four blank strips were set up in a fixture, we had to tack-weld them. They then went into the automatic welding machine, which had moving heads, and these welded only one side at a time. Now if you can only weld one side of a box section there are some inherent hot-and-cold problems, which tended to make the box twist. Hopefully, when we turned it over and welded the rest it tended to twist itself straight again!

Dropped into this chassis (not used, of course on the original prototype, which used a Jeep frame) was Rover's first-ever four-wheel drive transmission. It differed from that of the Jeep in many important features. The Jeep was normally used in rear-wheel drive form, and for off-the-road work the front-wheel drive propeller shaft could be clutched in to the transfer box and drop gears by means of a simple dog clutch, operated by a lever in the cockpit. If four-wheel drive was in use on metalled surfaces, therefore, front and rear axles were geared solidly together and the tyres had to scrub as well as they could.

Rover did not like the idea of enforced wind-up on roads, but also wanted to provide permanent four-wheel drive. To get the best of both worlds, therefore, and by using their own accumulated expertise, they inserted a freewheel between the transfer box and the front propeller shaft, which allowed the front wheels to overrun the rear when necessary.

Even though the project had top priority in 1947 (and it now seems clear that work on the Land-Rover delayed the P4 saloon car project by a few months), it was going to take a good deal of time to get the vehicle into production, and to get all the operating experience necessary in time for launch. Layout and detail design were completed remarkably quickly, and the very first prototypes owed a lot to the army-surplus Jeeps bought 'over the counter' by the engineers, but complete test vehicles were going to take much longer than this.

'Old Number One'—the very first pre-production machine, with chassis number R.01, which has been restored, and is part of the Leyland Historic Vehicles Collection

Rover therefore decided to short-cut the usual sequence of events—prototype, better prototype, pre-production, and finally off-tools machinery—and go straight for an early run of pre-production Land-Rovers. Building up the first vehicle of them all had taken about 6 weeks (it was the complex casting and machining operations to transmission casings which took most time), and the second followed a few weeks later. By this time the incredibly simple chassis welding method had been proven, a jig had been completed, and pilot production could begin in earnest.

The chassis jig, known by its operatives as a 'Christmas Tree' because of the number of bits and pieces sprouting from it, soon proved its worth. Before the Land-Rover was ready for announcement, twenty-five pre-production (or pilot-run) machines had been built, and another twenty-five were commissioned before the car went into series production in July 1948.

By the end of the summer of 1947, inside the factory, in the farmland surrounding the Solihull plant (which the company had prudently purchased a little while earlier), on Maurice Wilks' Anglesey estate, on other farms and in the most unlikely places, several stubby little machines, unbadged and unregistered, could be seen tackling any job

When a truck cab was fitted to 80in wheelbase models, there was little payload capacity left over. Note that this is one of the later 'exposed headlamp' models

previously left to a tractor to tackle—hauling, towing, ploughing, driving farm machinery, providing power for threshing machines or for circular saws—they certainly proved themselves enormously versatile.

Information about these pilot-run cars was, and might always have remained, sparse, if it had not been for the determined research carried out by Tony Hutchings of Hampshire in recent years. In 1976 Tony bought a rather derelict old example in Sussex which had not been licenced for twenty years, restored it painstakingly to its original standard, and discovered that it carried the chassis number R.04, which indicates that it was the fourth of the original pilot-built cars to take to the roads—or rather, to take to off-road conditions. I readily acknowledge the debt I owe to Tony Hutchings for the information which follows.

It seems that forty-eight pilot-run vehicles were built, out of the fifty originally planned (the other two sets of parts presumably were used up as spares to keep the complete vehicles going). None were actually registered by Rover when they were new (all the pictures I have seen show them operating on British trade plates) but all were registered before they were sold off in 1948–9.

There were differences between the pilot-run cars, which is only reasonable when the nature of the testing is considered. All of them, however, had galvanised steel chassis frames (a process not used on a quantity production basis), and some at least had integral front bumper bars welded (rather than bolted) to the chassis frame proper. Some were sold as new vehicles, whereas many were used extensively in testing, and sold off after launch as used examples.

No fewer than nine of the original forty-eight pilot-run cars—with chassis numbers ranging from R.01 to R.46—have been traced at the time of writing. Some of them are in magnificent restored condition, and it is to Rover's eternal credit that they now own the original pilot-run car, R.01. This model, in fact, is far from original in its fittings (many of which are replacements), which is hardly surprising. After a lot of hard work at Solihull, it was registered HUE 166 and sold off to a Warwickshire farmer, eventually being repurchased in 1967.

Both bodywork, steering layout and seating arrangements came in for a great deal of change at first. That extraordinary first prototype, with the Jeep frame, had central steering, a central driving seat and no doors (nor any real provision for them). The rear load platform surround, the front wings and the canvas hood arrangements were not

Batch production at first, in the summer of 1948, as the proper production line is assembled alongside. Every Land-Rover in this shot is right-hand drive

carried forward to the pilot-run vehicles. The front bumper, incidentally, was of the bolt-on variety! There was a one-piece glass windscreen.

By the beginning of 1948, the Wilks brothers were confident that their new Land-Rover would be an adequate stopgap, and that it would be saleable both at home (where there was an enormous pent-up demand for almost anything on wheels) and overseas. As already related, the company had not previously been active exporters, and did not set up an export department until 1945, so that many distributorships and concessions were having to be concluded with virtually no knowledge of the territories or the companies involved.

The vehicle was still not ready for production (as with the prototypes, so with the production cars, it was complex forgings and castings which really held Rover back—their own chassis jig, the 'Christmas Tree' could do its own job right away), but it simply had to be put on show at the earliest possible opportunity. There still had been no British motor show (the first post-war exhibition was scheduled for the autumn of 1948, which was far too long for Rover to wait).

The Brussels and Geneva shows came along early in 1948, just too early for Rover to prepare, so the Amsterdam show, an important international occasion scheduled to open on 30 April 1948, was chosen for the public launch of the Land-Rover. Two pilot-production machines were present, one on the stand, and one (a left-hand drive machine) in use as a demonstrator.

No one really knew how the world would receive the Land-Rover, certainly not Rover themselves, who had absolutely no experience in selling this type of machine. Their last foray into the world of commercial vehicles had been with a one-off tractor version of the spidery Scarab air-cooled machine of 1931, and nothing more was ever heard of that.

The British price, announced in April even though the Land-Rover was not ready to go on sale then, was to be £450. Because of the type of machine it was, there was no British purchase tax to pay. That price looks very little today, but in 1948 it compared, for instance, with £242 (basic price only) for a Ford Anglia, £395 for a Hillman Minx, £640 for a Jowett Javelin, and £845 for a Rover 'P3' 60; the

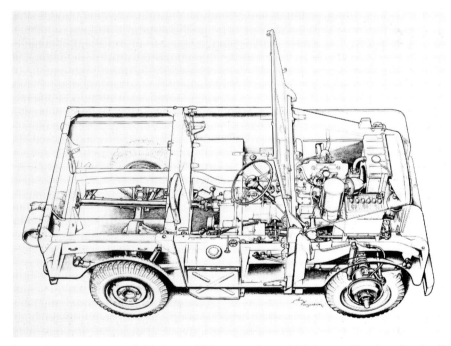

Land-Rover anatomy laid bare. This was the vehicle's specification in April 1948, when items like passenger seats, spare wheel and weather protection were all scheduled to be extras. The rear power take-off was fitted to the car drawn by the artist, but was also an extra

Land-Rover could not be compared directly with any of these, but then it could only directly be compared with a Jeep, which was not available in Europe.

Although that price looked reasonable—not forgetting that the Ferguson tractor had gone on sale in 1946 at £343, had soared in price since then, and was by no means a versatile road vehicle—it did not include a lot of equipment. As originally revealed, doors, side-screens, weather protection for occupants or payload, passenger seat cushions, heater, spare tyre and starting handle were all listed as extras. At least one got a spare wheel rim (without the tyre!), and a choice of left-hand or right-hand drive.

But was the Land-Rover good enough to fill up Solihull, and stabilise Rover's finances? The Wilks brothers hoped so, and thought they could sell at least 5,000 of them in the first full year. The Ministry of Supply, however, had other ideas. In December of 1947, when an original application had been made for an allocation of materials, there had been a grudging response of enough sheet steel to produce 1,000 Land-Rovers, which even then looked ludicrously low.

The new design could not possibly have been introduced at a more depressing time. If the design was right, the customers would appear, but if the materials were not available, the waiting lists would multiply. If the lists were too long, the customers would disappear in the end, and the Land-Rover would fail at the very beginning. Rover, its employees and its shareholders, could only hold their breath, and wait.

2 Land-Rover —
the Legend Evolves

The Wilks brothers need not have worried. Right from the start the Land-Rover's reception was enthusiastic. The press cuttings books still preserved at Solihull show just how much world-wide interest was generated by the premature announcement at the Amsterdam show. Not only in Britain and in Europe, but all over the world, motoring writers hailed the machine as a breakthrough.

In Britain, *Autocar*'s comments were typical:

> So much has been said and written in the past about the so-called People's Car, much of it nonsense, that the advent of a really practical British vehicle which goes far beyond that over-publicised proposal should be hailed with genuine acclamation.

Motor, too, had many kind things to say about this 'outstandingly interesting vehicle':

> It combines the go-anywhere properties already mentioned with many of the qualities of a light tractor, plus the added scope offered by a portable source of power which is available either for operating plant actually mounted on the vehicle, or for driving external farm or industrial machinery.

There was a mountain of additional comment in periodicals and newspapers, from staid financial publications to mass-market tabloids. All made it clear that they thought a new type of vehicle had been invented, that the world had been waiting for nothing else for years, and that the queues to buy would be enormous. The question of satisfying the demand became an immediate problem to Rover's management, one which they could not solve at first—and have not truly been able to solve ever since.

A big order book began to develop, not least from export territories. In a matter of days it became clear that original estimates of 100 sales a week would be exceeded at once, and even before production began it became clear that the word 'stopgap' would have to be erased from management's thinking. Because of the time it was taking to complete production tooling (even with such a simple design it was not possible to turn a good idea into quantity-production reality overnight), deliveries could not possibly begin before the end of the summer. The board's decision to go ahead with the Land-Rover project had been taken in September 1947, and in spite of post-war materials shortages the first Land-Rovers were on their way to customers within a year.

But if the demand for Land-Rovers was gratifying, the pattern of the orders themselves was rather disturbing. On the one hand it became clear that the stripped-down concept was not going to be popular, and on the other hand the customers lining up to buy the machines were not of the type envisaged. Further, Rover soon realised that people were not ordering Land-Rovers as tractor-substitutes, but as extra working machines to complement them. It is a measure of the design's versatility, and worth, that this did not harm its prospects one jot.

When the Land-Rover was announced, eighteen major extras had been listed, but it soon became obvious that seven of them—doors, sidescreens, driver's hood, passenger seat, spare tyre, spare wheel carrier and starting handle—would have to be standardised. To Rover's credit, this was done without raising the price, and deliveries commenced at £450, the same as that mentioned in April.

The Land-Rover was not a tractor. Maurice Wilks had never thought it was likely to be as efficient as a specialist farm appliance, though in fairness I have to admit that the original advertising mentioned its use as a 'four-wheel drive tractor'. Therefore, although prototypes had been set to farm tasks which included ploughing, hauling harrows and other implements around the land, it soon emerged that customers were more inclined to use their Land-Rovers as dual-purpose machines, on the road as much as off, for carrying a payload as much as towing a payload, and for transport as much as a full-time working machine. In particular its ability to use power take-offs and winches was invaluable to all its customers.

A feature of current Land-Rover production is the number of different body styles and engineering variations which can be seen on the same line, but in 1948–9 things were very different. There was only one body style—the 80in wheelbase machine with a canvas hood and an open back—and even the number of mechanical options was strictly limited. It all tied up nicely with the first Land-Rover concept —a very simple, very practical, 'stopgap'—but it did not accord with

Later in the 1950s the Land-Rover station wagon based on the 107in or (later) the 109in chassis was introduced. Though not as stylish as the 80in original, it was practical, simple to build, and became very popular. This is a 1955 107in example

the sort of enquiries the sales department were beginning to receive. Although the idea of a rugged little four-wheel drive machine, mechanically almost unbreakable, and with a corrosion-free body, was right, there were insistent demands for more.

Ironically enough, the very first 'different' Land-Rover developed was probably the least successful of all time, and this can be blamed fairly and squarely on its price. At the 1948 Earls Court Motor Show in London, Britain's first for ten years, an estate car derivative of the Land-Rover was shown. Still based on the 80in wheelbase chassis, which was given no mechanical changes, the estate car had a light alloy body shell, new doors with wind-down windows, and a two-piece tail-gate (upper and lower sections hinged at top and bottom respectively) which was to be used on other four-wheel drive 'road' Rovers in subsequent years. Four seats (two each side, facing into the centre of the body) were provided in the rear, making the new estate car a seven-seater, and it is interesting to note a quoted unladen weight of more than 3,000lb—400lb up on the canvas-hood version—which did nothing for the performance. Because of the body style employed, where the roof curved away from the screen, the estate car was several inches taller than the basic machine.

A detailed comparison between 88in (above) and 109in (below) Land-Rover rolling chassis shows the basic difference in frame layout. On the 109in machine there is a load-floor extension behind the front seats *and* behind the back axle. Ahead of the bell-housing the two layouts are identical. Note that the short-chassis machine has a 2,286cc petrol engine fitted, while the long-chassis has a six-cylinder 2,625cc unit

Although the new estate Land-Rover was a very practical machine, to the British legislature it qualified as a private car. Therefore, the customer not only had to stump up no less than £750 in basic price, but he also had to pay £209.08 in purchase tax—a total of £959.08. This was more than double the price of a canvas-top Land-Rover, and did absolutely nothing for the demand. Although the export price was free of purchase tax, the estate car version was still not an attractive proposition, as it was not only much more costly, but also rather slower and less economical than the original. It was eventually withdrawn in 1951.

With the Solihull production lines coming 'on stream' later in 1948, deliveries began with a vengeance, and the Wilks' dream of filling the echoing halls of Solihull was soon realised. Even in the first year of

The 86in Series I rolling chassis of the mid 1950s, with 1,997cc engine

its life, Land-Rover sales exceeded those of Rover's private cars (8,000 were built in 1948–9, 16,085 the following year), and within months it was decided that it should become a permanent feature in the Solihull scene. Development of the basic design, and its refinement, then went ahead.

In the next four years the original 'Regular' Land-Rover (as the canvas-hood version was always known) was to be joined by hard-top models, vans with windows, truck-cab derivatives, and a simpler and more basic seven-seat station wagon. As the expanding flood of Land-Rover customers invented more and more jobs for their new toys, so did the demand for more and yet more special fittings increase, and soon it was no longer practical to order a Land-Rover 'off the shelf'.

While all this was going on, one important mechanical change was made to the transmission, though this was phased in without public announcement. In 1950 the combination of permanent four-wheel drive and a freewheel in the front power line was discontinued; in its place came a transmission where rear-wheel drive was normal in high range, four-wheel drive in low range, and where four-wheel drive could be locked in for high-range driving. The freewheel was dropped completely.

Battered, but by no means bowed, this 88in model was air-lifted in to the Darien Gap to join the Range Rover expedition. There is no windscreen because it was snapped off in the first of several rolls!

This was done when the Land-Rover's average pattern of usage became clear. On sealed surfaces four-wheel drive absorbed power, even with a freewheel in the system, and was not necessary to provide adequate traction. The new layout, therefore, was as versatile as ever, and more efficient (which was good for the customers), while being simpler and cheaper to build (which was good for Rover themselves).

Although the Series I Land-Rovers were in production for nearly ten years (and about 200,000 were sold) the models being built in 1957–8 were considerably different from those originally put on sale in 1948. In that time the engine was enlarged once, a diesel engine became available, and a sum total of no fewer than five different wheelbase lengths were employed. Yet through and around all this the Land-Rover's principal philosophy—strength, versatility, simplicity, and indestructibility—was not changed. And from 1948 to 1958 the vehicles were recognisably related.

In almost every case the changes were dictated by the way customers were treating their machines. All, without exception, seemed to over-load their Land-Rovers, so it was natural that they eventually began to demand more powerful engines, and more payload space into which to cram yet more overload. It was the penalty of providing a vehicle which was demonstrably so willing to have a go at any job, whether or not it was truly meant to be doing so.

The first visual changes arrived in 1950, when the headlamps emerged from their hiding place behind the wire-mesh grille in the nose, and gave more adequate night-time vision at the penalty of some vulnerability to stone damage. For the 1954 86in model the facia panel was reshaped, the original modest-sized dials were discarded, and the familiar circular dials which were to be used for so many more years were adopted.

Even before anything was done to enlarge the physical capacity of the Land-Rover, steps were taken to improve the performance. It was not yet time to commit an entirely special engine design programme to the vehicle (that would have to wait until 1957), so this had to be done by enlarging the original engine. From the beginning of 1952, therefore, the 1,595cc unit was completely replaced by a 1,997cc engine, which was visually similar, but stronger and more powerful. Whereas the original engine had used a bore and stroke of 69.5 × 105mm, the revised unit measured 77.8 × 105mm.

At that moment there was no question of standardising the unit with a private car engine, as the obsolete unit had last been seen in the 1949 P3 model, while the new dimensions would not grace a P4 '60' until 1953. It is also necessary to point out that the 1,997cc engine first used in the 1953 P4 had an entirely different cylinder block, a light alloy cylinder head, and SU carburation. Not until 1955, when this P4 cylinder block was adopted for the Land-Rover, would some degree of interchangeability be achieved.

Although the engine's swept volume had been increased by 25 per cent, the maximum power output was only up from 50 to 52bhp. The benefit of the change was in torque, and low speed pulling power (which was also reflected in the ability to run power take-off equipment). Maximum torque was up from 80lb ft at 2,000rpm to 101lb ft at 1,500rpm, a nominal 26 per cent improvement made even more useful because it was developed at a lower speed. The Land-Rover now really had the sort of power unit to make it a 'go-anywhere, do-anything' working tool.

Demand for more load space had come from all round the world. Not only was it suggested that space in the 80in machine was too limiting, but that larger versions—larger, that is, by a considerable amount—would also sell well. The original Land-Rover, after all, was only 11ft long, and only 4ft of that was loading space behind the seats.

With the enlarged engine in production, therefore, and with the sales force now clamouring for larger and yet larger Land-Rovers, Tom Barton and his team were briefed to do something about this. With the Land-Rover selling so well, and with the project now commanding a dominant place in the company's future plans, these changes could be substantial. Two different models appeared, to replace the original one.

In short-wheelbase form, the 80in model was enlarged to 86in. Effectively these 6in were inserted between seats/bulkhead and back axle (relatively speaking, the axle was moved back by 6in) and there was an added bonus of 3in extra load floor behind the line of the axle. The load floor, therefore, was 9in longer than before. This sounds simple, and looks easy to arrange, but necessitated chassis side-member changes, new propeller shaft, revised bodywork (and all its variations), new springs and dampers (to look after the revised weight and payload capability), and many other details. The result of all this change was a noticeable improvement in carrying capacity, and an increase of more than 100lb in unladen weight.

Although a great deal of new material had gone into making the 86in Land-Rover, it was nothing compared to the effort which had to be directed at a long-wheelbase version, which began life with a 107in wheelbase. This was 21in more than the revised 'Regular' Land-Rover, and no less than 27in more than the original. Not only that, but to balance the style and the loading platform, the tail was lengthened yet again; there was an extra 41in of loading floor behind the seats which settled all the requests of customers and sales department once and for all.

To an engineer, a study of the 107in chassis layout is interesting. Although many details were shared with the 86in frame (brackets, some cross-members, and suspension pick-up points) the main side members were entirely different. Because of their greater length it was inevitable that new tooling would be needed, but in one very important aspect they broke new (or, rather, conventional) ground. They were still assembled by the extraordinary process of edge welding developed in 1947 for the first Land-Rovers; normal overlapping U-section steel pressings welded together were not adopted until the introduction of the Series III 109in model in 1971.

The 107in wheelbase machine was altogether bigger, heavier and more imposing than its ancestors. In basic form it was nearly 7ft tall

Lord Stokes being given a demonstration of the Series IIA's agility at a trade show at Stoneleigh. Is the driver threatening to park him up aloft until he agrees to more investment for the Land-Rover?

with the hood erect, and weighed in at 3,031lb. According to Rover's technical literature it was allowed to carry three persons and 1,500lb for road use, reduced by 300lb for cross-country use.

With some of the optional bodywork now being offered it was inevitable. One version now available was a ten-seater station wagon which, if loaded to capacity with healthy construction workers on a building site, would certainly be asked to lug up to 2,000lb around. What the company thought is not recorded; the Land-Rovers themselves rarely complained.

In Britain, on the other hand, the customs and excise authorities were very vocal. It was all very well, they said, for Land-Rovers to be sold free of purchase tax if they were used for carrying freight, and they even agreed that vans carrying people also qualified for exemption. Estate cars, whether working vehicles or not, were not Land-Rovers but *cars*, and should be taxed accordingly. It was a controversy which Rover could not wriggle out of, despite lengthy and diplomatic efforts. By one of those exasperating, if not endearing, quirks of British law, however, Rover had the last laugh. When the twelve-seater station wagon was introduced in 1962 (I realise it is not easy to cram twelve people into the confines of a Land-Rover shell, but such a model is marketed in considerable quantities), it became free of tax once more. These variants, Rover pointed out with legalistic truth, were not cars, but *buses,* and as such were commercial vehicles free of tax. Is it any wonder that the ten-seater was speedily dropped from the home market once the price advantages of the twelve-seater became obvious?

But was the Land-Rover a private car, a commercial vehicle, or an agricultural machine? It was a question which would have taxed the best brains (who would probably have answered: 'All three'), and it was much more than a philosophical nicety. In Britain, at least, a great deal of motoring and commercial law depended on the definition being made. Not only was there the question of purchase tax to be settled, but there was that of depreciation allowances for business use, and those connected with insurance and related details.

In Britain, two major problems related to the speeds at which a Land-Rover could be driven on the open road, and to the type of petrol which should be used. Up to 1951 petrol for private use was rationed, and two types were supplied—one for private use and one dyed red for business vehicles. 'Red' petrol was only supplied against the appropriate type of petrol coupons, and it was a heinous offence for a private motorist to be found with 'red' petrol in his car's tank.

How, then, should a farmer or businessman fuel his Land-Rover, when it might be used for all purposes? Unless he was rich, indeed, he might have to use it as his tractor *and* as his car. There was much consternation over this issue, usually glossed over by local police forces who knew the individuals concerned, and in any case the problem was resolved when rationing was abandoned.

Whether or not the Land-Rover was a commercial vehicle, and in what forms, was a major issue, and of great importance to its customers. In Britain commercial vehicles were speed-limited to

30mph, even on open roads, and although a Land-Rover could never be classified as a performance machine it was a lot faster than that. The problem was that the police and the judiciary were loath to let Land-Rovers have it both ways. If it was to be taxed (or, rather, *not* taxed) as a commercial vehicle, surely it should be driven as one. In short, as a trade-off for the financial advantages, the police thought it should be used accordingly.

What is really amazing is that the Land-Rover had been on the British market for eight years before its status was finally settled, and even then the solution would have done Solomon proud. After many simple prosecutions for speeding had been won by the police, in 1956 the persistent Mr C. Kidson from Wareham in Dorset (who had been fined the princely sum of £3 for speeding) took his appeal all the way to the Appeal Court for the matter to be resolved. In a very important judgement, Lord Chief Justice Goddard ruled:

Mr Kidson was driving a modern type of Land-Rover which was more like a truck. It could carry passengers in the cab and goods in the back, but it was capable of being used as a four-wheel drive vehicle, and this brought it within the definition of a dual-purpose vehicle. It was not, therefore, subject to the 30mph limit on goods vehicles.

When the powered trailer was in use behind the 101in Land-Rover, the result was a 6 × 6 machine with phenomenal traction and hill-climbing abilities

The original Road Rover of 1952, with its crude but effective estate car body. Not without reason, it was always known as the 'Greenhouse'. If you look carefully, there is evidence of Series I Land-Rover body panels being used, notably in the front wing/bonnet area

The Land-Rover, except in closed-van form, where speed limits still existed, was therefore cleared, and it is fair to say that even the harassed police forces breathed a sigh of relief. But the court ruling emphasises what a breakthrough Rover, and the Wilks brothers, had achieved in designing the Land-Rover, for it had completely ignored all previous standards and conventions, and had really established a new type of motor vehicle altogether.

True pioneers usually find that their trade mark is taken up to describe the copies which inevitably follow. The Land-Rover, after all, only had to follow the Jeep, which was unknown in many countries where Land-Rover exports began at the end of the 1940s, and it soon became the generic name for all such four-wheel drive machines. Austin, for instance, have always complained that their Gipsy was known as the Austin 'Land-Rover' and provided free advertising for their opposition. Thinking up another name for the machine (because commercial advertising was absolutely forbidden on the air) proved very difficult for the BBC, especially after the Queen took delivery of a special example, and often appeared in news film in it. They eventually settled rather weakly for 'field car', but even that pretence was dropped after a few years when the very name of Land-Rover had become a standard word in the British language.

Two years after the introduction of the 86in/107in Land-Rovers, another change was introduced, and on this occasion Rover were at pains to make as little of it as possible. The change, introduced in the autumn of 1956, sounded simple and trivial enough. It was no more and no less than a 2in increase in both wheelbases—to 88in and 109in respectively—and might have been dismissed as unnecessary if the reasons behind it were not known.

Because they were not yet ready to reveal their true motives, Rover carried on churning out vehicles with the new dimensions, but from June 1957 it all became clear. For a number of years they had been working on a new light diesel engine, which was unavoidably bulkier than the existing petrol engine, and the extra 2in were needed to accommodate it. The extra 2in had been inserted in the chassis ahead of the toeboard and behind the line of the front axle, and if this had been detailed in 1956 the reasons would have become clear.

Demand for a diesel engine had been channelled through the sales force's market studies, and was growing all the time. There were many commercial fleet customers whose *only* petrol-engined vehicles were Land-Rovers, and in some parts of the world it was much easier to locate supplies of diesel fuel than petrol.

Thinking about a new engine design, however, was considerably easier than actually providing one. Even in the 1950s, when prices were much lower than today, and when there were no restrictions on exhaust emissions and noise to push up development costs and times, it still needed multi-million pound investment to ensure big supplies of a new engine. Although Rover could possibly have bought a diesel engine 'off the shelf' from the Perkins company of Peterborough or even from another car-making concern in the motor industry, they preferred to do the job themselves. This meant that factory space would have to be found, new transfer line machine tools would have to be ordered, a lot of precious capital allocated, and diesel-engine experience built up from scratch,

We did not realise it at the time, but the diesel engine which appeared at first was only one part of a master plan for prolonging the Land-Rover's life. The new engine family was conservatively expected to last for at least twenty years, and there would be both diesel and petrol-engined versions. Although there would be obvious major differences between the two, certain vital dimensions (cylinder bore centres, block height and length, and many other details) would be shared, so as to reduce the capital cost of developing two new engines. For not only had the directors decided to provide a diesel option, but they had decided to replace the existing P4-based petrol engine with a new and even more rugged unit.

The mysterious 2in were explained in June 1957 when the new diesel engine was announced, though many must have been equally as perplexed by the strange cylinder dimensions (2,052cc, 85.7 × 88.9mm bore and stroke) which denoted an entirely new range of engines from Solihull. It was the first new design since the i.o.e.v. layout (in four-cylinder and six-cylinder form) had been revealed in 1948, and even that had been designed late in the 1930s.

The design was new from end to end, and top to bottom. Valve gear was perfectly conventional, with a line of vertical valves in the cylinder head, push-rod operated from a camshaft mounted in the offside of the cylinder block. Fuel injection was by CAV equipment, and there were swirl chambers in the head, allied to pistons having small combustion chambers cast into their crowns. Both block and cylinder head were made in cast iron. A feature of the cylinder block was that slip-fit wet cylinder liners were used. This allowed ample cooling water to circulate around the bores, and meant that engine renovation would be cheap and simple when bore wear became excessive. The whole unit looked rugged, and ready to run for ever.

As one might expect, the new diesel engine was not as powerful as the petrol-powered unit, nor did it develop as much torque. Maximum power was 52bhp at 3,500rpm, and maximum torque 87lb ft at 2,000rpm (compared with 52bhp at 4,000rpm and 101lb ft torque at 1,500rpm for the petrol engine).

All these improvements—engine boosts, alternative power units, wheelbase increases, and more and yet more body options—had all been achieved without altering the Land-Rover's essential simplicity, without requiring great capital sums to be spent, and without impairing the ease with which large numbers could be built. Production had first passed 500 vehicles a week in 1954, and was still on its way up. In every way it was a very profitable product for Rover to have in its range.

None of this had gone unnoticed by the company's competitors. They had seen the ease with which the Land-Rover had established itself, they had noted the growth of waiting lists, and had envied the way in which Land-Rovers seemed to be virtually indestructible. They

Road Rover in its final 1957 form, with split tail-gate, curved glass rear quarters, and a modified P4 chassis. The car had not been completed when this picture was taken. A P5 instrument board was due for fitment to the facia

had also seen the way—as the pioneer—the Land-Rover name had also become the hallmark of the 4×4 breed. In short, the competition was becoming jealous, and intended to do something about it.

By 1956, even before the final wheelbase stretch, and before the diesel engine option had been introduced, Rover's management had heard that the Land-Rover was soon going to have to face up to British (and possible European) rivals. If management were not worried (they were extremely confident in the Land-Rover by then), they were at least concerned about their product's future. Was the Land-Rover good enough to face up to competition without change, or had it had matters too easy for a while?

It is not easy to decide that a world-wide success needs change, especially when total sales were racing on towards the 200,000 mark and the queue to buy new ones was longer than ever. But the directors were not complacent. They decided to approve something which to a Land-Rover enthusiast could almost be called heresy—they decided to let the stylists have a look at it!

3 The Go-anywhere, Do-anything Machine

The records show that the Series II Land-Rover was launched in April 1958, and it is no coincidence that it closely followed the release of Austin's Gipsy, which had appeared in February. But no new competitor, and no earth-shattering event, brought the Series II project into the world. A combination of pressures, submissions, and management decisions (taken in 1956–7) helped to bring matters to a head. That said, there is no doubt that the existence of the new Gipsy added urgency to the process.

In the past it has been suggested that the Series II models were brought out hastily once the imminence of the Gipsy had been detected, but this is not so. Even in the motor industry of the 1950s, when design was not so hampered by legal and safety legislation as it is today, it took a long time to get new ideas into production. As ever, engineers had long lists of improvements ready for approval, merchandising staffs continued to reflect their customers' demands, and product planners tried all they knew to divine their rivals' intentions.

Although it was not the only reason for going ahead with the Series II Land-Rover, the Gipsy *was* a useful catalyst. Other factors, not least the news that other firms were looking longingly at the 4 × 4 business, hastened a reappraisal of the Land-Rover's place in the market. The Willys Jeep, though mainly sold in North America, was beginning to find substantial markets in overseas territories; Fiat had produced their first Campagnola models, and even the Japanese (still an unknown force) were rumoured to have such things in mind.

Even before this, however, there had been commercially significant pointers. In 1954 Spencer Wilks had heard that Willys-Overland had been casting around for a European partner to help them establish a Jeep factory on this side of the Atlantic, and after he had started merger discussions with Alick Dick of Standard-Triumph he was shocked to learn that Willys had already been in touch with the Coventry concern. These talks between the two British firms, incidentally, centred on the possible advantages of marrying Rover's

Land-Rover assets with Standard's tractor-building reputation, and developing new engines and other components to suit both concerns. The talks broke down within weeks, principally because it is believed that Rover became disillusioned with Standard's financial performance and prospects. It did not help that Alick Dick's parting comments were that if the two companies could not achieve a merger, then Standard might have to consider building a 4×4 of its own . . .

Tom Barton, now director of Land-Rover product engineering, but then merely a section leader in the Land-Rover design offices, also recalls that one of his senior colleagues (Mr Cullen) was attracted away to David Brown industries in Yorkshire, where he was to design a new 4×4 machine, and that he (Tom Barton) was also invited to make the move as well. 'As you can see,' Barton told me, 'I stayed, but later Colonel Pogmore, my boss, was invited to join BMC at Longbridge to look after the design of the new Austin Gipsy, and he asked me if I would go with him!'

With senior staff moving on to take charge of new and secret projects like this, a rival firm's intentions become clear very quickly. Austin's plans had therefore been uncovered before their tooling orders had been placed.

The 110in forward-control Land-Rover, which was based on a normal control 109in chassis frame. It had a most useful payload capacity, but for all that was not as versatile as the more normal Land-Rovers

After the piecemeal development of the Series I Land-Rover, which was still going on as ideas for the Series II model began to crystallise, it was time to go in for a serious rethink of the entire concept. While everyone now appeared to be happy with the choice of wheelbases (88in and 109in, indeed, have remained as the normal-control machine's wheelbase dimensions ever since their introduction in 1956), there was engine work to be done—and it was time to pay attention to the looks.

In the beginning, the Land-Rover had never been subject to the attention of the styling engineers. Its body had been devised solely with an eye to practicality, and to simplicity. Yet no other 4 × 4 machine, not even the very successful Jeep, had been conceived in such a basic way; all, to some extent or other, had been shaped with attraction to line in mind. Even in this strictly utilitarian market, therefore, the Land-Rover could move forward with the times, and submit to some cosmetic attention from David Bache's styling department.

For Bache and his artistic engineers, this was an entirely new challenge. They had just completed work on the big 3-litre P5 saloon car, with its big expanses of leather, real wood, and high-quality fittings—shaping the revised Land-Rover could not possibly have been a bigger contrast.

Legend has it that when PininFarina were asked to advise on a

Forward-control Land-Rovers had impressive cross-country ability, helped by excellent traction and a huge ground clearance

reshaping of the VW Beetle in the 1950s they could suggest nothing more than a revision to the rear window opening. Bache's problem with the Land-Rover was equally difficult. As he once commented some time ago about this task:

> The Land-Rover (as we found it) was so absolutely 'right' already that we couldn't just dash in with some obvious improvements. It just wasn't the sort of machine that cried out for decoration, and because of the nature of its work there was no point in putting in a lot of delicate shape into the panels.

It is worth noting that when the Range Rover was being shaped about ten years later the same criteria did not quite apply. Although the Range Rover is still essentially a two-box shape it is by no means slab-sided, and every skin panel is produced by press tools. Perhaps, one day, in the 1980s or 1990s, even a Land-Rover might take on the same aspect?

Visual changes proposed, and accepted by management, were subtle and practical. The most glaring deficiency to a stylist was the way in which the chassis frame and exhaust system was exposed in side view, and a simple 'modesty skirt' was added under the doors and wings to disguise this. Front and rear wings and doors were all reshaped so that a touch of 'barrel side' was introduced; this was no more than a suggestion, and the panels could still be produced without the use of enormously expensive presses. Inner wing and inner door structures were not changed. A little more shaping for the bonnet panel completed the actual sheet metal improvements, though the doors began to look more like private car doors and less like an exhibition of the casting engineer's art. On some models the fuel filler neck was now accessible from outside the body without the doors or seat cushions having to be moved.

Inside the cockpit there were concessions to driver comforts, with pendant pedals offering easier movements, and with sprung (though hard and flat) seat cushions and back rests for the first time. On the 109in models the driver's seat could be adjusted, and it was possible to order a floor carpet. Inner door panels were trimmed and there was glass instead of perspex in the sliding sidescreens.

Although the basic chassis engineering was not changed, wheel tracks were increased by 1.5in, and minor improvements to the front axle allowed the turning circle to be reduced by 3ft for the 88in model, 5ft for the 109in. Rear springs were now hung from the outside of the chassis frame rather than directly under it, and this helped to provide an extra 2in of wheel movement.

The most important mechanical improvement was to the engine line-up. New for the Series II (though subsequently fitted to some older Series I machines by their owners) was an overhead valve 2,286cc petrol engine. This was in no way related to the existing 1,997cc engine, as even a casual look at cylinder head, valve gear, and machining details makes clear. Close inspection, in fact, proved that it had much in common with the 2,052cc diesel which had been on offer in Land-Rovers since the summer of 1957. However, apart from the obvious functional differences (cylinder heads and fuel supply arrangements were unique to each type), the new petrol engine had a conventional cast-iron cylinder block without cylinder liners, but still with cooling water around these bores. It will be recalled that a feature of the diesel derivative, which had a narrower bore, was that slip-fit wet liners were specified.

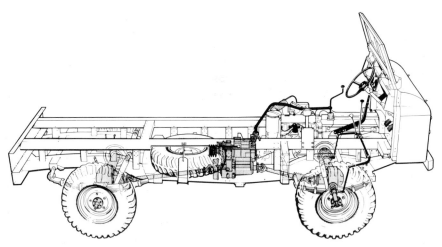

Look carefully at this 'ghost' sketch of a 110in forward-control Land-Rover, and you will see the normal-control 109in frame forming the basis of the structure. This particular example has the 2,286cc petrol engine, but diesel or six-cylinder alternatives were also on offer. Note the gear change extension

Although the i.o.e.v. 1,997cc engine was supposed to be dropped when the model change took place, this did not happen at once, and a considerable number of 88in models of the Series II type were built with the 1,997cc engine during 1958. This was done merely to

The cockpit of the forward-control Land-Rover looked normal—as it should have done, for most of the production cab and seating layout was employed

balance stocks and building programmes, and the anomaly was rectified in the autumn when the last of the 1,997cc units was fitted. At this point, therefore, the Land-Rover's engine links with P4/P5 saloon models were broken, though they were to be rejoined in 1967 in a rather different way.

The announcement of the 2,286cc petrol engine now made the considerable investment in a new diesel engine look more sensible, as the two units obviously stemmed from the same basic design, and shared many common components. Both engines shared the same crankshaft stroke (and, therefore, the crankshaft machine tooling). The petrol engine had a bore and stroke of 90.47 × 88.9mm (in Imperial measurements that was $3\frac{9}{16} \times 3\frac{1}{2}$in), compared with 85.7 × 88.9mm ($3\frac{3}{8} \times 3\frac{1}{2}$in) for the original diesel.

Not only was the new petrol engine larger than the old unit, but it was considerably more powerful, and at this point I should pause to summarise the power output situation so far:

	Engine	Bore/stroke	Power/rpm	Torque/rpm
1948–52	1,595cc	69.5 × 105mm	50 @ 4,000	80 @ 2,000
1952–8	1,997cc	77.8 × 105mm	52 @ 4,000	101 @ 1,500
1957 on	2,052cc Diesel	85.7 × 88.9mm	52 @ 3,500	87 @ 2,000
1958 on	2,286cc	90.47 × 88.9mm	70 @ 4,250	120 @ 1,500

In ten years, therefore, the Land-Rover's petrol engine had grown by 43 per cent, maximum power had risen by 40 per cent, but maximum torque (the benchmark by which its usefulness as a *machine* was measured) had shot up by 50 per cent. Though a formidable working vehicle when announced, the Land-Rover in Series II was now a really outstanding prospect for almost any task.

It is very interesting, too, to compare the movement of prices between 1948 and 1958. Britain, like most industrialised countries, had suffered from inflation, though not on the same scale as was to occur in the 1970s. On the other hand, the choice of Land-Rovers was wide and far-reaching.

At home, therefore, we must compare the single 80in Land-Rover, in Regular form, and selling for £450 in 1948, with this range in 1958:

88in	Regular	(2-litre petrol)	£640
88in	Regular	(2-litre diesel)	£740
109in	Basic	(2¼-litre petrol)	£730
109in	Basic	(2-litre diesel)	£820
109in	De Luxe	(2¼-litre petrol)	£750
109in	De Luxe	(2-litre diesel)	£840
107in	Station Wagon*	(2-litre petrol)	£815 + £408.85 purchase tax

*The 107in Station Wagon was a Series I carry-over model which was dropped later in the year.

The price of the Regular model, therefore, had risen by 42 per cent in the ten years of production, which was broadly in line with the increased power and working capacity which it offered, and certainly no more than private car prices had suffered in the same period.

This, then, was the new model which the company had begun hinting at a few weeks earlier, with the rather convoluted and obvious catchphrase: 'When better Land-Rovers are made, the Rover company will make them'. It was a *better* Land-Rover, faster, more rugged and even more versatile than the original, and more stylish into the bargain.

It also had to face competition in Britain from the Austin Gipsy, which was what all the fuss was really about, and it is now time to consider this newcomer, and compare its engineering. The Gipsy, on hindsight, has to be judged a commercial failure, though Tom Barton recently summed it up succinctly and accurately:

There was a lot wrong with the first Gipsys—it was as if they had been designed by people who didn't understand the sort of life a 4 × 4 had to lead—and this gave them a bad name from the start. But, to BMC's credit, they worked away to make it better. Funnily enough, by the time the Gipsy was dropped in 1968, it was a good product. We were quite relieved to see it go!

At a casual glance, the Gipsy of 1958 had a lot in common with the Land-Rover philosophy, but there were important differences. Like the Land-Rover, the Gipsy had a choice of petrol and diesel engines, it had four-wheel drive, and the now-conventional arrangement of high and low ranges with rear-wheel drive only normally being in use for on-road motoring. It was fully competitive on price (£650 for the petrol version, £755 for the diesel), and it was backed by BMC's huge distribution network. On the other hand, it had three features which

The strangest Land-Rover of all? As modified for the RAF. Although tank-type half tracks are employed, they are driven around pressed-steel wheels and normal car-type tyres. To say the least, the handling was exciting. It is *not* true that bomb disposal (this vehicle's purpose) was carried out merely by driving over the bombs!

could not be reconciled with Rover's experience—only one wheelbase (90in), four-wheel independent suspension, and pressed-steel bodywork.

Tom Barton invented a Land-Rover saying, many years ago, which is still apt: 'Off road performance is limited by the comfort of the driver.' He is referring, of course, to the stiff ride given by the suspension over rough ground, and the way this throws the driver around. Tom Barton goes on to say: 'A leaf spring suspension is the best way I know of getting a driver to be cautious over rough ground, and therefore avoid needless damage to his vehicle. If you make the ride very soft, people drive even harder over rough ground, and they might tend to break things faster.' Which explains the Gipsy's early problems, in part.

The Gipsy's Flexitor trailing link suspension used rubber in torsion instead of steel springs, and it meant that the front and rear differentials were chassis mounted, with articulated drive shafts to each driven wheel. This seemed to bring all manner of service problems with it, not least the fact that although the wheels pounded up and down on rough terrain the differentials did not, which made them and the centre transmission case rather more vulnerable to damage.

The fact that only one wheelbase was available at first was presumably due to the practical difficulties of making a complete range at the same time, but there could have been no excuse for adopting pressed-steel bodywork. One of *the* biggest selling features of the Land-Rover was its corrosion-proof light-alloy body, which was both light and easy to produce. By choosing steel for the Gipsy, Austin made a rod for their own back, and the vehicles soon got a name for speedy deterioration.

In later years the Gipsy became more serious opposition. Hardtop and station wagon versions were announced, a long-wheelbase option (111in) was added in 1960, and 'Land-Rover' types with rigid axles and half-elliptic leaf springs were offered from autumn 1962 (though an 111in hybrid with Flexitor front suspension was also offered, as a halfway house from one design to the other). Even so, it was never a strong seller, and was withdrawn at the beginning of 1968, soon after the Leyland-BMC merger had been announced. There can be no doubt that the two events were connected—it made no sense for a new corporation to have competing 4×4 ranges in production, and there was no doubt as to the most popular.

No matter what the competition, at home or overseas, the Land-Rover continued to be a fast seller. The number of options and alternatives increased, until Solihull could, if it had wanted, produce different

Enormous tractor wheels, fitted front and rear, make this special Land-Rover useful for floating over swamps and across big ruts on forestry commission territory

Land-Rovers for weeks on end before it had to repeat itself. More than 28,000 Series II models were built in the first full year of production. A year later this achievement was topped, with 34,168 being built, and with the quarter-millionth machine being built in November 1959. Production figures kept on increasing (though the factory, the original 'shadow factory' building, was bursting at the seams) and the first 1,000 per week achievement came in 1965, 17 years after the Land-Rover had first been announced, and just months before the half-millionth model was built.

Rover's delicious problem was not that they had no competition, but that the Land-Rover continued to prove that it could tackle almost anything, anywhere in the world. Sales staff stopped being surprised by the odd-ball pictures they received, or the weird requests for modifications. George Mackie, in charge of the department which formalised the approval of certain conversions on the Land-Rover chassis, must have wished for a more quiet life.

Nevertheless, development of improvements continued. Only a matter of three years after the arrival of the Series II range, it was replaced by modified Land-Rovers known as Series IIA models. This was not a very dramatic change, and there was absolutely no way to distinguish one type from the other. Not even under the bonnet was there any obvious change, but a look into the technical specification told a different story. The original '2-litre' diesel option (actually 2,052cc) had been dropped, and replaced by a dry-liner 2,286cc diesel engine, which had the same bore and stroke as the petrol engine and was therefore able to share even more components and machining facilities. In bald terms this meant that the diesel versions now came with 62bhp at 4,000rpm, and maximum torque of 103lb ft at 1,800rpm, compared with 51bhp and 87lb ft respectively.

Compared with 1958, too, prices were up again, though not by much. The 88in Regular machine with petrol engine sold for £672 (£640 in 1958 with the last of the 2-litre engines), while a 109in example with the optional diesel engine cost £875 (£840 in Series II guise in 1958).

In 1961 both Series IIA Station Wagons listed—88in and 109in—with seven and ten seats respectively, were burdened by British purchase tax, but from May 1962 a twelve-seater version of the 109in machine became available. As already mentioned, in Chapter 2, under British law this device then qualified as a passenger-carrying bus, and did not have to pay purchase tax or any other sort of tax. Further, because all Land-Rovers had been classified as 'dual-purpose' vehicles since that famous test case of 1956, the new 'bus' was not speed limited like most other machines of this type. The twelve seats were arranged as follows: three in the cab (including the driving seat), a row of three foldaway seats across the body immediately behind the front compartment, and two rows of three seats along the sides of the body facing inwards.

Customers were therefore faced with an easily-solved dilemma—whether to pay £1,293 for a ten-seat station wagon (petrol-engined), or to pay only £950 for a twelve-seater? In basic price the extra two seats cost a mere £10, and there was a popular diesel-engined alternative for an extra £110.

About this time, slowly and steadily the Land-Rover began to become civilised. Competition, and customers' usage patterns, started

Twin axles and a special rear chassis frame to increase the carrying capacity of this Series IIA Land-Rover

to force this upon the engineers. There was no need for a wholesale redesign, nor for striking good looks, but perhaps it *was* time to pay more attention to creature comforts than had once been the case.

The pattern of customer usage had been clear for some years. As already mentioned, the Wilks' original idea of a Land-Rover which could double as a tractor never seems to have materialised. Nevertheless the vehicle could be (and invariably was) used on and off the highway, on and off sealed tracks, and in the most amazing variety of situations. To see a Land-Rover hauling a trailer full of pigs (or manure, or hay bales, or feed sacks, or calves, or logs, or working implements, or whatever) was normal, and to be expected. But had the Wilks brothers expected to see Land-Rovers hauling luxurious caravans, to see them become motor caravans, or to see the county and horsey set take them up as ideal dual-purpose machines? Had they ever expected to see Royalty reviewing troops and guards of

For use at Le Mans in 1965, this very special forward-control Land-Rover
was given kneeling rear suspension, and front-wheel drive only, so that the
Rover gas-turbine car could easily be loaded and transported to the circuits

honour from the back of specially-converted models? Had they ever
expected customers to buy more than one Land-Rover at once—one,
in effect, for farm labouring, and one for road use?

These trends, and the challenge of competing 4 × 4 models brought
out in North America, Europe and the Far East, eventually led to an
entirely new type of vehicle from Solihull—the Range Rover, which
was also an evolution of the Road Rover prototypes of the 1950s—
but in the meantime the gradual smoothing down of the utilitarian
Land-Rover began.

There were two important features to be studied. The driving compartment had to be made to look more like that of a private car, and
another engine option, offering more power *and* refinement, had to
be found. The question of providing creature comforts was tackled
with great circumspection, and for years was limited to little more
than the choice of optional 'luxury' seating. That of providing the

Land-Rover with yet another engine was more fundamental, and, in a way, more difficult.

Even in the 1960s, when the Land-Rover was an acknowledged money-spinner at Solihull, it rarely attracted the investment capital that it deserved. There always seemed to be a new Rover private car —P6 (the '2000'), or the vee-8 engine project, for instance—which had more urgent need of the available funds. Tom Barton's team, therefore, had little choice when they came to modify the design to take another engine. They could consider any available engine (and, at this time, remember, they were not associated with any other firm who might have provided a possible engine), but they could afford neither the time nor the expense to design a new one.

Even though William Martin-Hurst had secured the rights to manufacture the lightweight General Motors vee-8 in Britain, there was no way it could be available in quantity before 1967, and at that time every engine produced would be earmarked for the P5 and P6 private car ranges. Jack Swaine, in charge of Rover engine design for so many years, once told me that he was briefly allowed to dabble with the idea of designing a cast-iron vee-6 engine which could be machined on the same transfer tooling as that being laid down for the new vee-8, but that this was cancelled in the face of considerable extra tooling bills. The idea of using the Rover 2000's new 1,979cc four-cylinder engine was also considered, but once it was realised that some de-tuning would have been needed to provide it with a suitable torque curve, and that this de-tuning would not have left the unit much more powerful than the existing special 2,286cc unit, this project was also cancelled.

The only alternative, therefore, was to consider one of the P4/P5 'sixes' which were still being made in considerable quantity at Acocks Green. These engines, of course, were closely related to the four-cylinder units fitted to all Land-Rovers built between 1948 and 1958, with the same unique i.o.e.v. valve gear and sloping cylinder head/block joint face. Although they were quite considerably longer than the 2,286cc petrol/diesel engines it was thought that space could just be found for their inclusion.

Although the design had been started in the late 1930s, and the engines had been in production since the late 1940s, they had a splendid reputation for reliability and refinement. By 1964, when the last of the P4 saloons was built (and, therefore, spare engine-building capacity became available) two sizes—2,625cc and 2,995cc—were

Messrs Dixon-Bate, of trailer hitch fame, devised this Land-rover/trailer combination, based on a cut-and-shut Series II 88in chassis

current, both with seven-bearing crankshafts and a single SU carburettor.

Shoehorning the longer 'six' into the restricted confines of the Land-Rover structure was not easy, as the main body panels had to remain unchanged, while for obvious reasons the position of the main transmission case and transfer gear had to be unaffected. All the extra length, therefore, had to be accommodated by letting the engine 'grow' forward.

Clutch and bellhousing space were reduced to an absolute minimum, and to everyone's intense relief it was found that there was just enough space. To suit the Land-Rover requirements the 2.6-litre version of the engine was chosen, and de-tuned somewhat. In private car form it had been good for 93bhp (net) at 4,750rpm in '95' form; for the Land-Rover application, in de-tuned form with a reduced compression ratio (7.8 or even 7.0:1 for certain territories), and a big oil-bath air-cleaner, it produced 85bhp at 4,500rpm, with maximum torque of 132lb ft at 1,500rpm. This, of course, and all the silky power delivery for which the Rover saloon cars were so famous.

The six-cylinder engine was only ever made available in the 109in chassis (not because it could not be fitted in the 88in chassis, which was identical in dimensional terms in the engine bay as the 109in, but because of handling reasons, and because the sales staff wanted it that way). Compared with the 2,286cc petrol engine it cost a mere £60 more, a considerable bargain reflected in its immediate popularity.

At the same time the cockpit was slightly revised, as part of the rationalisation process. This modification was introduced simultaneously on all Land-Rovers. Instruments were restyled, switches and minor controls were grouped together on the central facia panel, and the old separate starter switch was finally displayed by a combined key-operated ignition/starter switch. A single wiper motor, with concealed rack near the base of the screen, replaced the original individual wiper arrangements, and the hand brake was extended and reshaped to make its operation more convenient. It was also an appropriate juncture to convert the entire electrical system to negative earthing, a process then being standardised throughout the British motor industry.

Announcement came in April 1967, and there was barely a criticism in sight. *Autocar* carried out their own test appraisal in July 1967 and were very complimentary about the twelve-seater station wagon they assessed. The tester, thought to be Stuart Bladon (now that august publication's Deputy Editor) had many caustic things to say about the law relating to twelve-seaters, but nothing but praise for the new engine installation.

Between 1962 and 1970 the strangest-looking Land-Rovers of all were the forward-control models which were in production at Solihull. Although these vehicles used many standard Land-Rover components, they are so different—in basic layout and in looks—that they merit separate description.

The forward-control models were developed because Rover management wanted to extend the limits of their range. Although the normal-control Land-Rovers were (and are) wonderfully versatile, and were excellent working machines, there was no doubt that the conventional placing of engine, transmission and driving compartment limited the amount of useful space for stowing goods or passengers. When the design staff were asked to develop a Land-Rover with a 30cwt payload capacity, and a bigger load space, the only obvious solution was to consider forward control.

What evolved was not really a Land-Rover, not of the type that the world knew, but more of a light truck. There was only one basic version, with a three-seater open or truck cab, but it had an enormous 10in of ground clearance, and with such a high nose and tail it could deal with phenomenal changes in surface profile without grounding.

Work started in 1960, and the first example was shown in public at the 1962 Commercial Vehicle Motor Show in London. It was so obviously based on the Land-Rover, but equally obviously very different from it, that most observers had a good look at the chassis engineering to see how it was all done.

The forward-control machine's wheelbase was 109in, which gave an immediate clue to the basic layout of the chassis. Sure enough, inspection showed that the new vehicle's chassis incorporated the bare bones of the existing normal-control 109in frame, to which a complete additional top framework, providing a flat loading platform, had been bolted. Old and new frames were securely buttressed together, were enormously stiff and torsionally rigid, and formed an ideal basic structure for the new vehicle. The solution was undoubtedly heavy, perhaps too heavy for its purpose, but was simple and could be developed with the minimum of fuss. The alternative, which was to develop an entirely new frame and chassis layout, would have meant committing more development and production capital than could be afforded at the time.

There was only one engine on offer at first—the normal 2,286cc petrol unit in its usual state of tune. Engine and four-wheel drive transmission were in their conventional places relative to front and rear axle lines, which meant that the Land-Rover assemblies could be used. Heavy-duty axles were adopted (they would later be useful when the 1-ton Land-Rover was being designed) and the tyres were a massive 9.00–16in.

Rover publicity claimed that more than 75 per cent of the normal-control machine's parts were used in the forward-control Land-Rover. Even the cab was a cut-about version of the usual cab, but remounted well forward, on the nose of the new chassis frame. The biggest problem for the engineers was in rearranging the steering layout and the gear change linkage—along with details like the throttle control and various other cable runs.

In this form the rolling chassis complete with cab sold for £948, and the whole machine complete with dropside body cost £1,015. Naturally there was no purchase tax to be paid.

The original forward-control Land-Rover was not a success, probably because it was somewhat under-powered if a full payload was carried, and probably because *total* demand for that sort of commercial vehicle (for such it undoubtedly was) was quite limited. Although a variety of intriguing specials (described in Chapter 4) stemmed from the forward-control vehicle, not least that attractive *front*-wheel drive Le Mans car transporter, a redesign was needed to give it more appeal.

This was completed in time for announcement in 1966, and included a minor increase in the wheelbase (to 110in, with the front axle moving forward on its springs by 1in), and with 4in wider wheel tracks (to 57.5in) along with a front anti-roll bar, to improve the handling and stability. More important was that a choice of three engines was now available—the 2,286cc four-cylinder units, in petrol or diesel form, and (for the first time in a Land-Rover) a six-cylinder 2,625cc petrol engine, already described when fitted to the Series IIA Land-Rover. Strangely enough, although the 2,286cc petrol engine had been the only one available on the original forward-control machine, this was the only engine *not* made available in Britain on the revised model. In six-cylinder form the price became £1,215, while the diesel-engined version sold for £1,282.

Thus revised, the forward-control range carried on until 1972, when they were effectively elbowed out of Solihull by the much more specialised military forward-control chassis, which was an entirely different and more sophisticated design. A study of this vehicle is reserved for Chapter 6 which deals with military Land-Rovers.

In the meantime, however, the refinement process had been carried a great deal further, and was leading to the still-current Land-Rover range. For Rover, 1971 was a very important year.

4 Specials and Expeditions — the Impossible Takes a Little Time

It is a long time since I was surprised by the extraordinary jobs which could be tackled by a Land-Rover. If not in strictly standard form, but in specially-prepared guise they can be asked to perform the most unlikely-sounding duties, and produce the most prodigious results. Two important features—the remarkable traction offered by the four-wheel drive transmission, and the almost unbreakable structure—account for this.

Could any other vehicle in the world, for instance, be used as a shunting locomotive on standard-gauge railways, provide the basic framework for an experimental crop-spraying hovercraft, be the mounting platform for conversion to four separate caterpillar tracks, form the basis of an armoured military scout car, be used for refuse collection, operate a snow plough, or be the motive power under sets of aircraft baggage loading equipment?

I once asked a senior executive at Solihull if there was any really important job which Land-Rover had not yet tackled? He paused, looked thoughtfully into the distance, then commented: 'We haven't seen a Land-Rover on the moon yet, which is reasonable because there's no air up there to let the engine work!' There was then another pause, a gleeful grin, and he added: 'But if someone could supply another power source, a Land-Rover would be very useful up there, wouldn't it?' I do not think he was joking.

As far as I know, Land-Rovers have not yet penetrated to the North or South Poles, but on the assumption that their engines could be started in that forbidding environment they could be the world's only alternative to a tracked vehicle. They do, however, appear to have worked almost everywhere else. Land-Rovers are known to spend their useful lives deep underground, working in mines. They operate in extreme climates (as hot as it comes in the Middle East, or as cold as almost anywhere in the world in Canada). They are found in some of the most unwelcoming work sites in the business (can anyone really enjoy building oil terminals in the Shetlands in winter?) It is quite

Although this was conceived as a gimmick, it worked very well, and floated effortlessly across sown crop fields. Most of the power, however, went into getting the modified Land-Rover up on its skirts

usual to see Land-Rovers delivering the mail in remote parts of the country. You would expect to find a Land-Rover working for its living on almost any farm, but what about routine police use in the middle of a city?

The engineers at Solihull rarely make specially-modified vehicles unless they are exclusively for factory use. On the other hand, so many intriguing ideas are, or have been, submitted to the company for approval, that a special department has been in existence for years to cope with them. George Mackie who looks after all matters relating to such projects, and the proprietary approval which may follow from his engineers' complete assessment of a scheme, agrees that the flow of schemes shows no signs of stopping.

Mackie was one of the originators of the Rover-based Marauder sports car (along with Peter Wilks and Spen King) in the early 1950s, but returned to Solihull in due course when that project was closed down. His department opened at the end of the 1950s, and is now a

A much-modified forward-control Land-Rover in use by the Road Research
Laboratory in the 1960s

vital clearing house for special vehicle conversions, equipment and
accessories proposed for Land-Rovers and Range Rovers.

A couple of years ago, Mackie's department produced a masterly
survey of the function and scope of the Proprietary Approval Section,
and (with his approval) I now quote a few extracts from the historical
survey with which the document opens:

> Activity which may benefit from proprietary approval . . . is brought
> about by the fact that 4×4 vehicles are deliberately designed with
> versatility and workhorse capabilities in mind . . . it may help to draw
> on the analogy of the tractor. Basically a tractor is useless until it is
> attached to a piece of equipment to which it can supply the required
> operating power . . . 4×4s differ in two significant respects from
> tractors. Firstly, they are useful in their own right as transport . . .
> secondly, 4×4s, or those which have separate chassis frame type of
> construction, are in demand for special body conversions in a manner
> unavailable to tractors.

. . . In the Land-Rover activity we had a situation where on the one hand engineering departments were engaged in product improvement and future design, which have their own peculiar complexities, and on the other hand dealing with a demand for technical help and advice from equipment manufacturers and specialist body builders.

. . . To overcome this the 4 × 4 Special Projects Section was formed in Engineering to look after and control this activity.

Special Projects were never short of work, and there is always a fascinating variety of strange-looking 4 × 4s parked outside George Mackie's office at Solihull; on my last visit pride of place went to a massive three-axle six-wheel Range Rover chassis, by Carmichaels of Worcester, with a high-performance fire tender installation and the obligatory bright red colour scheme. With such an impressive rig, a siren almost seemed superfluous.

The fittings offered for approval can be as small as a new type of winch or power take-off, or as comprehensive as the complete conversions now so familiar in local authority, civil defence, or nationalised industry hands. When Mackie's survey was prepared at the end of 1976, the author was able to quote (in round figures) the approved conversions which had been built since the department opened and these included:

2,000 fire fighting units	2,300 motor caravans
1,000 self-propelled compressor units	800 mobile workshops
	750 elevating platforms
3,000 ambulances	500 crop sprayers
1,000 mobile cinema units and outside broadcast units	300 armoured cars
	250 chassis extensions
5,000 vehicle recovery units	

And there were many more specialised, and less numerous, vehicles. Mackie also goes on to quote something known to Solihull's sales department for many years: 'In the opinion of several of the manufacturers of these items, sales would have been from 15 to 25 per cent greater had vehicle availability been better.'

Not quoted in the list of equipment sales, which is headed by the statistic that more than 5,000 sets of freewheeling front hubs (which, potentially at least, improve fuel consumption when in use on sealed surfaces), is mention of the overdrive kit, which is now an important option fitted to Land-Rovers after assembly.

Startling by Land-Rover standards was this revised facia and instrument layout, introduced on the Series III Land-Rover from 1971. In no way was the practicality of the machine affected

Fairey Winches Ltd, who manufacture this overdrive unit, went through the entire proprietary approval process, and can now offer a kit which can be fitted to a Land-Rover by any competent dealer in no more than three hours. It is not an overdrive in the Laycock sense (which uses epicyclic gears and a feature of clutchless engagement or disengagement), but is nothing more complex than an extra two-speed gearbox mounted on the tail of the transfer gearbox of the Land-Rover, by a housing bolted to the existing transmission case.

It is, in all respects, a modern gearbox, with synchromesh engagement of one or other of the sets of gears, but with control by a separate lever which is positioned on the transmission tunnel near the Land-Rover's three existing levers. In direct drive there is no torque passing through the overdrive box (the input gear is locked direct to the main shaft), but in overdrive the torque goes through the train of four gears before being fed back into the transfer gearbox. The step-up ratio thus equipped is $0.782:1$, and there is a definite if not sensational improvement in fuel consumption. There are no physical or torque limitations on the use of the overdrive, which means that a Land-Rover owner can grapple with the possibility of sixteen forward gears (all with synchromesh engagement), and with no less than four reverse ratios.

This sort of equipment—overdrives, freewheeling hubs, winches, power take-offs and the like are the most popular—is the hidden way in which one Land-Rover differs from its neighbour. Air-conditioning installations have been approved, snow-clearing sets tried and found satisfactory, and 'extras' like luxury seat packages eventually proved to be so popular that they were incorporated in the specification of later models. The assembly of a new Land-Rover, incidentally, is by no means the standard process it might appear. When the order is placed (*all* Land-Rovers are built to order—no one at Solihull can remember a time when any of their 4 × 4s were built for stock in standard form) it lists options, extras and special instructions, apart from making the choice between engines, of wheelbase lengths, of body types, and of colours.

It would be rather meaningless to list the number of Land-Rovers which could be built to different specifications before two identical examples are inevitable. One only has to think that the choice of options starts at ground level, with different makes, types and sections of tyre, proceeds through a choice of spring and damper settings, encompassing the choice of conventional or freewheel hubs on the way, and the potential complications become clear.

In so-called 'standard bodywork' (standard because the factory build them) there is still a big choice of fittings. Open and truck cabs, canvas tilt or van rear sections with or without side windows, side-hinged or top-and-bottom hinged tail gates, station wagons, chassis/cab versions and chassis/front bodywork versions for completion elsewhere, all feature in the lists. No fewer than twenty-seven different variants were listed in 1978, though the advent of the V8 Land-Rover will now have altered this somewhat.

Scores and scores of equipment options can then be added to the order, which may be as major as the specification of the complex hydraulic power take-off or a simple request for ashtrays or sun visors to be added at the assembly stage. It is simple and straightforward to ask for towing hooks, locking filler caps, or fire extinguishers to be fitted, but it is also feasible for engine oil coolers, tropical roof kits, steering dampers, power-assisted brakes and even low-ratio transmission transfer gears to be specified. No wonder that when I asked how

R.01, the first pre-production Land-Rover, poses with a 1973 example to commemorate twenty-five years of Land-Rover production. The site is the Long Mynd, in Shropshire

quickly a cancelled order was taken up a production controller laughed out loud. 'It would be impossible,' he said, 'to find another order exactly like the one which had just been cancelled.' But then few people cancel their Land-Rover orders; they know that to lose their place in the queue might cost them a year's delay.

When the Land-Rover, therefore, reached its twenty-fifth anniversary in 1973, Rover felt quite justified in dubbing it 'The World's Most Versatile Vehicle', and anyone having the privilege of thumbing through the company's Salesman's Manual would no doubt agree.

The illustrations in this book can give only an idea of the many special conversions offered from time to time on the basic Land-Rover chassis. Some, like the hydraulic elevating platforms grafted into the back of truck-cab versions, still look recognisably standard. Others like the armoured cars can only be spotted by careful reference to wheels, basic dimensions, and the existence of the Land-Rover badging which the specialist may have retained.

One of the most interesting of all was the factory-developed racing-car transporter which evolved from a prototype 1½-ton forward-control truck which had been built for Ministry of Defence appraisal, and was

Optional 'luxury' seating package, later standardised, on the Series III used to carry the Rover-BRM to and from racing circuits. Not only did this have its four-wheel drive installation converted to front-wheel drive only, along with the use of constant velocity universal joints in the hubs, but its track was 5ft 6in, and a Perkins 5-litre diesel engine was used. It was also provided with special 'kneeling' rear suspension so that the gas-turbine racing car could be eased up to the carrying platform on very gentle ramps.

It was the factory, too, which converted one of the new Series IIA models to flanged wheels, so that it could be used on British Railways sidings, towing (in a most publicity-conscious manner) a string of trucks loaded with normal Series IIA ready for delivery. Its real purpose was to produce a dual function rail/road vehicle for the transport of permanent way maintenance equipment and personnel. Its use as a shunting 'locomotive', however, was little more than a gimmick, as a bit of thought into the loadings and the pitfalls will reveal. Overcoming the inertia of even two trucks was enough to give the standard clutch a hard time, and braking them to a halt was almost guaranteed to bring on fade in the linings and heart failure for the driver. British Railways were reputed to be interested, but I feel they were only being polite; their smallest shunting locomotives, after all, dispose of at least 200bhp.

Some of the uses for specially-modified Land-Rovers are due to their exceptionally effective four-wheel drive system. This goes right back to the original Maurice Wilks theory that a Land-Rover should be as good as a tractor. Land-Rovers working over slippery ground can even be improved by the fitting of special tyres. Rover themselves offer sand and swamp tyres, but the British Forestry Commission obtained even more phenomenal results by modifying examples with huge tractor wheels and tractor tyres, front and rear. This involved wholesale changes to the bodies, but it allowed a Land-Rover to climb in and out of vast ruts produced by earth movers, and trenches dug into the earth for the trees to be planted.

One of the most ungainly, and at the same time most beautifully modified, was the 109in wheelbase example once assessed by the British Royal Air Force, which had tank tracks added in place of each of the normal wheels. The resulting device sat very high off the ground, as pivoting sub-frames were added to each wheel position, with the tracks spaced out around full-size wheels with normal tyres attached, two to each 'wheel' position. Viewed from the side, this astonishing machine sat on two triangularly disposed tracks, with four wheels inside the tracks at each side of the car. Unlike other such tracked vehicles, normal steering was possible. Normal vehicle steering was aided by an engine driven pump and power steering. It was also astonishingly easy to complete this conversion. A day's work was all that was required to mount or demount the sub-frames and convert the vehicle to a normal Land-Rover again.

Four-wheel drive, too, is invaluable in a vehicle used for crash recovery, or for towing jobs which may involve heaving a car out of a ditch or accident situation. Specialists make a lot of those, as George Mackie's figures suggest, and any number of 'breakdown' Land-Rovers have been privately converted by garages when bigger, older and less efficient four-wheel drive trucks have expired.

It also explains why such a hard-sprung vehicle should find such wide use as an ambulance. Personally I would not fancy being transported far, in a delicate condition, in a Land-Rover ambulance, but if this was the only sort of vehicle which could reach me (perhaps across ploughed fields, unmade tracks, or impenetrable scrub) I would not quibble very much. It is in such conditions that a Land-Rover ambulance has, quite literally, saved many lives. Fire tenders, by definition with a limited supply of foam and powder, also succeed for the same reasons. If they have to make their sure-footed way to a fire which defeats all efforts of conventional appliances to reach them, then they are providing a vital service.

In many other cases the Land-Rover structure is a useful, and perhaps ideal, clothes-horse for people to carry out their special conversions, and in this case the separate feature is the key to the design. Light-duty articulated truck rigs have often been built on an 88in Land-Rover chassis by mounting a trailer or special fitting to the modified frame in true 'artic' style. Ordinary flat-bed trailers, horse-boxes or even exhibition pavilions have all benefited from the treatment.

Land-Rovers can tow caravans, but they can also become self-contained motor caravans. As is the case with Land-Rover ambulances, a Land-Rover motor caravan is most attractive to the customer who wants safe and secure living quarters built into the four-wheel drive capability of the Land-Rover. On adventure holidays, or the sort of trips where civilisation disappears for weeks at a time, and solid surfaced tracks are just a fond memory, to carry one's home on one's back is extremely reassuring.

Even before the most outlandish Land-Rover 'specials' were invented,

Neat and practical motorised caravan conversion by Carawagon, and specially prepared for an expedition with stowage for extra fuel, and extra stores above and ahead of the cab

the vehicle was beginning to make a name for itself on world-wide expeditions. Whether it was for personal exploration or in a group, whether for pleasure or with an exploring purpose, whether privately or publicly financed, expeditions soon discovered the versatile qualities of Rover's 4×4, and it was not long before Solihull was being inundated with requests for complete Land-Rovers, extra equipment for Land-Rovers, financial sponsorship towards the projected trip, help with the preparation of the vehicles, or a combination of all these.

In the beginning a few—a very few—applicants were lucky, but once it became clear that the Land-Rover had already forged its own impregnable reputation, and that virtually nothing new was to be learned from sending factory-sponsored Land-Rovers to yet more outlandish territories, no more assistance was granted. In its place, the factory sat down and produced a little booklet called *A Guide to Land-Rover Expeditions* which is at once helpful and amusing, practical and whimsical, and contains a great deal of basic, perhaps even life-saving, advice. The booklet is still not widely circulated, and I make no excuse for quoting a few snatches from its twenty-two pages.

For instance, there is advice on the type of Land-Rover to choose, and even the engine to be chosen: 'A station wagon or hardtop will not only be more dust-proof, but with locks and security catches fitted, pilfering is made more difficult.'

They make the point that there are more advantages to the choice of a petrol engine than of a diesel engine, including: 'Petrol is a cleaner fuel than diesel, and less pungent.'

It also says much for the faith Land-Rovers have in their products, and the service network which exists all over the world, that this is said: 'It cannot be over-emphasised that the further away from civilisation the more difficult and expensive it is to obtain spares.'

And what about these comments:

Front-mounted jerricans should not be used to carry fuel due to fire hazard in the event of an accident. . . . Never wrap your thumbs around the steering-wheel rim. If the vehicle hits an obstacle the steering-wheel could be jerked so hard that the spokes could catch and break your thumbs. Many people have learnt this the hard way. . . . (Regarding photography) remember, in some countries even the most innocent of buildings or structures can be classed as 'of strategic importance'. . . . Don't forget the toilet rolls . . . the danger of snake bite tends to be exaggerated. . . .

The best of all, in the author's opinion is:

A convenient way of washing clothes whilst travelling is to put them in a waterproof sealed container in the back of the vehicle with a suitable amount of water and washing powder. After 100 miles they should be clean!

By the end of the 1950s, a Land-Rover had taken part in nearly every important expedition, and had penetrated to the far corners of the earth. It is worth recalling that the Army's feat in defeating the Darien Gap in 1972 was not the first time that a Rover 4 × 4 had struggled through that inhospitable region. During the spring of 1960 Richard Bevis and Terry Whitfield tackled the Colombian jungle alone in their Series II 88in Land-Rover, and accomplished the passage in 134 days. By alone I mean that there were no other vehicles in attendance, but as Bevis's own account in *Autocar* of December 1961 stressed: 'On 3 February 1960 we edged nervously into the dark decaying fringes of this silent world, with our group of thirty men armed with machetes, axes and a power-saw . . .' It was a trip not without enormous frustrations. The participants claim to have blazed 310 miles of trail through a virgin and hostile jungle, built 125 palm log bridges, forded 180 rivers, built three rafts for floating the Land-Rover across unconquerable patches of water and suffered ninety punctures. This was claimed to be the first-ever crossing of the Darien Gap by a wheeled vehicle. No one has ever come forward to offer evidence of earlier expeditions.

A couple of years later a heavily-sponsored Chevrolet expedition got through with three rear-engined Corvairs, but the author simply refuses to believe that this was feasible unless the cars were towed much of the way, or even modified with four-wheel drive. In any case, the Range Rovers which repeated the trip in 1972 were considerably quicker than both previous expeditions, but had more mechanical trouble, and were helped a great deal with much more military support. It is extremely significant that over the years there has been no rush of imitators to prove the worth of their own 4 × 4s, and the achievement has certainly never been devalued by later successes.

When the Army decided to undertake a two-fold job in 1974, of proving the worth of pre-production forward-control 101in Land-Rovers, and of getting a good deal of publicity in the process, their dilemma was not in finding a journey which would test the new design to the full, but of finding one which had not been rendered meaningless by repetition or the progress of civilisation. There was no point, for instance, in tackling, say, a north to south passage of Africa, even if the Sahara was still a formidable challenge, for a ludicrously ill-organised World Cup Rally had devalued that expanse of sand in the spring of 1974, and to extend the trip all the way to Cape Town would have been to invite arrest by unfriendly governments on the way, and to have the precious new Land-Rovers impounded.

For the lack of almost any other newsworthy choice, it was decided to tackle the entire width of the Sahara, from west to east, starting from the Atlantic coast at Dakar and finishing on the Red Sea in Egypt. Because there were so few dramas, this successful quest was something of an anti-climax, except that the 101in machines (four of them, two being equipped with Rubery Owen powered trailers, to give a 6 × 6 capability) coped with great aplomb and reliability. The entire trans-Sahara expedition took 100 days, which, for the 7,500 mile journey meant an average daily sector of 75 miles, and average fuel consumption was sometimes as high as 5.7 mpg. The biggest problem, at times, was that there was an almost complete lack of petrol supplies, so the Army—like snails—had to carry their houses and supplies along with them. After all, 1,200 miles without fuel needs a considerable reserve of the precious fluid, and it was here that the trailers proved to be invaluable.

The impossible takes a little time? Indeed it does, but in the case of the Land-Rover the 'impossible' is usually a case of finding an impossible journey for it to tackle. Many of the old 'impossible' journeys have now been completed by 4 × 4s, often Land-Rovers, and in modern times they are only repeated with the object of breaking some nebulous speed record or other. It is yet another indication of the way Land-Rovers, and their competitors, have opened up the world to the ever-curious human being.

5 Now, on to the Second Million . . .

It is with the release of the Series III Land-Rovers that this story really begins to come up to date. Series III models have now been on the market since late 1971, record numbers (well over half a million) have already been built, and the vast expansion programme now going ahead at Solihull and elsewhere is intended to make further technical improvements feasible, and for much higher rates of production to be achieved.

There is nothing revolutionary in this big scheme. As many managers at Solihull have told me, it could have been approved years ago, but has repeatedly had to be postponed. This was not because there were fears that more Land-Rovers could not be sold (the long waiting lists prove otherwise) but because other more urgent demands for capital spending had to be dealt with first. Even after British Leyland effectively became a nationalised concern in 1975, and after the British government had promised major funds for modernisation and expansion, the Land-Rover was left to struggle on in its crowded and outdated facilities.

It was not until 1978, in the aftermath of yet another financial and political upheaval at British Leyland, that Land-Rover Limited was set up as a separate (and very profitable) concern. Only then was the much-rumoured plan for doubling Land-Rover/Range Rover production approved. The first benefits of this work, to cost £280 million when complete, have already been seen with the launch of the V8-engined Land-Rover in 1979 and many more exciting developments are in the pipeline.

Nevertheless, what is now happening at Solihull, for consolidation and further growth throughout the 1980s, would not have been possible if the Land-Rover had not been such a consistent money-spinner in the 1960s and 1970s. It was the major step forward from Series IIA to Series III Land-Rovers, one of the first of Rover's development programmes to be approved by the board of British Leyland, which laid the foundations.

However, so much was going on, commercially and financially, in the 1960s, that I should now summarise a few important dates, company developments, and factory changes.

Late in the 1950s Rover had begun development of a new private car (coded P6, and later to be named the Rover 2000); it was formally decided to put this into production at the October 1960 board meeting. The problem was that new buildings would be needed to accommodate an increase in total production—either in which to make the new model, or into which Land-Rover production could be moved. For a time there were several alternatives, one of which would have meant moving Land-Rover assembly to a brand-new factory at Pengam, near Cardiff. In the end an entirely new building at Solihull (which has always been known as the 'North Block') was erected to house Rover 2000 production. P5 assembly would continue in the 'shadow factory' building, alongside the Land-Rover building, as would the P4 range, but it was expected that the last of the P4s would leave the factory in 1964. Land-Rover assembly would then stretch itself, but not much.

Now on to the second million! The 'Millionth Land-Rover' ceremony of June 1976, with the Mayors of Solihull and Cardiff present to give the specially-painted 88in 7-seat estate car a send off

Rover took over Alvis, of Coventry, in 1965, and there might have been scope for future expansion in that direction, if the big merger between Rover-Alvis and Leyland Motors (who already owned Triumph) had not occurred in the winter of 1966–7. By then more than 1,000 Land-Rovers could be built in a trouble-free week, and management were gratified to learn that Leyland would approve of further expansion. Then, in January 1968, came the last, and the greatest merger of all—Leyland joined forces with British Motor Holdings, which meant that (in private car terms) Alvis-Rover-Triumph were to be brought together with Austin-Morris-MG-Riley-Wolseley-Jaguar. BMC's commercial vehicles, tractors and the Gipsy would now have to live in harness with AEC, Albion, Leyland and the Land-Rover range. After that, and in great haste, rationalisation and joint policy-making got under way.

Rover managers were soon delighted to realise that British Leyland's management did not propose to meddle with the Land-Rover, nor did they try to integrate it with other products and insist that new production arrangements be made. Instead, they approved investment in the up-market Range Rover project, which would be announced even earlier than Rover had originally hoped, and they agreed to plans which would allow up to 1,400 Land-Rovers to be built every week. Further, they approved of outline plans then taking shape for the way Series IIA models should evolve into the Series III range.

In the meantime, the refinement and detail improvement process which had intensified earlier in the 1960s continued. Soon after the six-cylinder versions became available, export-market Land-Rovers began to be built with one important visual change—with their head-lamps mounted in the front of the wings, instead of in their familiar position close to the radiator grille mesh. This had been made necessary by certain new overseas market legislation, which concerned the maximum distance a main driving lamp could be from the outside of a vehicle. This change came in 1968, and as similar legislation was also pending in Great Britain, the same modification was then made to home-market and all other Land-Rovers in February 1969. No further visual changes (apart from the new nose style of the V8-engined Land-Rover) have been made since then.

For many years customers had been overloading their Land-Rovers, and were often taken aback when Rover pointed out that subsequent chassis and transmission failures could hardly be blamed on their machines. It was to satisfy them, and to stretch the range that important

bit further (to aid the 'conversion manufacturers') that the ultra-rugged
'1 ton' Land-Rover was offered from the autumn of 1968. Although
this variant of the design *looked* identical to other 109in machines,
it used the heavy-duty transmission components first developed for the
forward-control Land-Rovers, which had much more pronounced step-
down ratios. In bottom gear, and with low range engaged, this gave
a staggeringly-low ratio of 55.3:1. This much lower overall gearing,
necessary to make the carrying of heavier payloads a practical possibility,
was only partly offset by the use of the largest possible tyres—9.00–16in
—which were also needed to deal with the extra load, and give better
flotation.

The '1 ton', of course, referred to the normal maximum payload
approved for this new version of the design. The fact that 109in
customers were already habitually carrying more than this load (what
is the weight, after all, of twelve passengers in a Station Wagon?) was
not mentioned in company literature, and I have no doubt that this
limit, like the previous ones, was cheerfully ignored by the buying
public. The '1 ton', as it is always known, does not sell in large
numbers, but has proved to be a very valuable addition to the range.

Finally, in the autumn of 1971, the Series III Land-Rovers were
announced, and these vehicles are of course still in large-scale production at Solihull. Following the trends already made public in the
Range Rover style of 1970, these machines were a major and more
civilised improvement over all previous Land-Rovers. They were the
result of a major investigation into the world's 4 × 4 market and the
changing needs of customers.

Every aspect of the Land-Rover—mechanical design, basic model
range, options, equipment, and styling—was investigated thoroughly.
Naturally it would have been nice to contemplate an entirely new
model (the basic design, after all, had been on sale for about twenty
years when the Series III redesign began, and would have been on
sale for twenty-three years when the announcement took place), but
there were practical limitations to the amount of investment capital
which could be committed, and it was also clear that most buyers *liked*
the Land-Rovers they were already being offered.

New frames, new wheelbase lengths and new suspensions were
therefore ruled out (more and more Rover staff had come to believe
in the Barton maxim about driver discomfort). Even the basic choice
of body styles, and the general mechanical layout, would remain
unchanged. In detail, however, much could be done.

Central to the change was the revised transmission. Right from the start, in 1948, Land-Rovers had been sold with a strong, dependable, but essentially basic gearbox, having no synchromesh on first or second gears. Now, for the 1970s, and in spite of what Land-Rover enthusiasts thought about the old models, this box was to be thrown away. In its place a much revised gearbox would be fitted, with synchromesh on all forward gears, revised internal ratios, and a reduced low range step-down ratio.

This box was (and is) unique to the Land-Rover Series III range, having nothing in common with Range Rover or Rover private car designs. Compared with the old box, it had much lower first and reverse ratios; when combined with the less-pronounced low range step-down ratio this left the Land-Rover's house-side hill-climbing capabilities unaffected. Although it was an all-synchromesh design it was by no means as slick and smooth as a private car design. There were, and remain to this day, critics who ask if the change was really necessary. Rover would say that the change to all-synchromesh also included the use of helical constant-mesh gears, which are much quieter than the original type, that the 'gate' is much improved, and that it was necessary to bring the machine at least into line with its competitors. At the same time, incidentally, a diaphragm spring clutch was specified, and much reduced the operating efforts.

The range of engines was not changed, though alternators replaced the dynamos previously fitted. Bigger and better brakes were specified, and a vacuum servo was standardised on the 109in machine when fitted with the 2.6-litre six-cylinder petrol engine. Equally important to the industrial users who might not want to go the whole hog and order a '1 ton' was the fact that the heavy-duty rear axle and the stronger stub axles were now to be standardised on all 109in Land-Rovers.

The most obvious, if not the most significant, changes were visual. Although the styling engineers had been allowed to have yet another look at the Land-Rover's external style, they had concluded that changes either had to be minimal, or that they should be allowed to design a completely new (and, almost by definition, more costly) shape. Accordingly, the only obvious external difference between the last of the Series IIAs and the first of the Series IIIs was the new radiator grille mesh.

In the cab, for the first time since the beginning of the 1950s, there was a major restyle. Gone were the days when a Land-Rover had a couple of round instruments, two separate wiper motors, crude quadrants for opening air vents, and some exposed wiring and switch gear. In its place was a nicely integrated instrument and facia panel, 'handed' for left-hand or right-hand steering, complete with an open oddments compartment *and* provision for a radio to be fitted. A new steering-wheel, column switchgear, and a steering lock for territories which demanded it, all added to a new and smooth overall effect. Another aid to creature comfort was a $4\frac{1}{2}$kW fresh-air heater, which replaced the 3kW 'fug-stirrer' of previous Land-Rovers.

By comparison with any earlier Land-Rover, if not by comparison with the Range Rover, which was now in production at Solihull, this was an astonishing update of a previously utilitarian design, but it was no less than the changing market had demanded. The three-abreast seating could still be simple or 'luxury' according to the customer's wish, there were still knobs and levers in profusion on the tunnel, and there was no loss in practicality in regard to pedals and controls, but the Series III was undoubtedly a 'softer' design with even wider appeal than before. In the 1950s, for instance, who would even have thought of offering a Land-Rover customer the choice of a car radio? Would *any* Land-Rover, for that matter, ever be considered quiet enough for a radio to be truly audible? It was all indicative of the way in which the Land-Rover 'market' was developing; even with the Range Rover on the market—a product admittedly aimed at the upper end of the 4×4 business—a great number of Land-Rover buyers were wanting to carry out their business in reasonable comfort.

Prices were higher than those of 1971 Series IIA models, mainly because of the continuing (and accelerating) inflation in Britain, and only partly because of the better specification offered by the Series III. The basic line-up, including the Range Rover, was:

88in	with 4-cyl petrol engine	£1,002
88in	with 4-cyl diesel engine	£1,135
109in	with 4-cyl petrol engine	£1,185
109in	with 4-cyl diesel engine	£1,318
109in	with 6-cyl petrol engine	£1,263
88in	seven-seat Station Wagon (with 4-cyl petrol engine)	£1,511 (including British purchase tax)
109in	twelve-seat Station Wagon (with 4-cyl petrol engine)	£1,463
100in	Range Rover (with vee-8 petrol engine)	£2,134 (including British purchase tax)

Because of the vagaries of the British tax structure, an 88in seven-seat station wagon was rather more expensive than a 109in twelve-seat wagon. In export territories, of course, this anomaly did not apply, which explains why the seven-seat wagon remained in production, and why the 10-seat version on the 109in wheelbase was still available.

Compared with the very first (1948–9) Land-Rovers, the price of the simplest version had now risen by 123 per cent. Even compared with the first Series IIAs of 1961 (which started from a base-line price of £672) the rise was 49 per cent. It was a handicap which Rover salesmen could have done without, but it did not seem to hamper demand for Land-Rovers at all. Production continued to be limited by the facilities at Solihull and Acocks Green, but the waiting lists grew and grew.

It is interesting to know what the private car motorists thought of the latest Land-Rover, and *Autocar*'s comments on the 109in six-cylinder machine with a truck cab and canvas tilt are illuminating:

There were few adverse comments on the cab interior, which proved draught-proof and was trimmed to a standard unheard of in Land-Rovers a few years ago . . . It is amazing where the Land-Rover will go, even in two-wheel drive and high gear . . . The limits in this case are set not by what the vehicle will take, but by what the crew can take . . . It soon becomes second nature to ride the Land-Rover like a horse in these circumstances, and the seats play almost no part in the comfort or otherwise of the proceedings . . . As long as the ground is dry there seems to be no limit to what the Land-Rover will climb in low ratio first gear. It will certainly go beyond what the average driver's nerve will stand. It can also be taken *across* a steep slope with impunity, tilting a long way from the horizontal with no risk of falling over. . . . The one thing which can stop a Land-Rover is a long enough stretch of really deep (i.e. more than axle deep) mud. The only thing to do in this case is stand off and charge. . . . The feeling that it will go where nobody else can follow is curiously comforting, even if one can rarely take advantage of it. . . . It is hardly surprising that, twenty-three years after its introduction, Rover cannot meet the demand for the Land-Rover.

Autocar, too, is the only authoritative source of independent performance figures for the modern Land-Rover. This particular test showed that the 109in machine with 2.6-litre engine was only capable of 69mph (slightly more than 70mph downwind), that it took 31.7 seconds to accelerate up to 60mph, and that its overall 'on-the-road' fuel consumption was a miserable 14.9mpg (using two-star fuel). Even at a constant 30mph its fuel consumption was no better than 19.4mpg, which showed that the frictional losses in the transmission were equally as critical as the effects of that vast and bluff frontal area on aerodynamic flow.

Thus rejuvenated, the Land-Rover strode on to more and more sales, bigger and more widespread reputation, and an insatiable demand for more to be built. The three-quarter millionth machine had been built in June 1971, just before the Series IIA was faded out in favour of the new Series III models, but it was the Series III which was to be the subject of the much-publicised 'Millionth Land-Rover' occasion.

In one way—but only one—the 'Millionth' example was a bit of a cheat. By keeping a close touch on the production figures, Rover knew that the true millionth machine was due at the end of May or beginning of June 1976. On this occasion, however, they had decided to make the occasion more memorable than before. The 'Millionth' example, therefore, was scheduled as a very special 88in seven-seat station wagon, with the ubiquitous 2,286cc petrol engine but with many of the more popular extras fitted, and was actually built a couple of weeks before the milestone was reached.

Even before the Solihull ceremony of June 1976, when the car was once again rolled off the final assembly line in the presence of Solihull and Cardiff civic dignitaries, Press and TV cameramen in some profusion, it had been the star of the Thames TV *Drive-in* motoring magazine programme, which also featured R.01 (the 1948 pilot-build car) and one of the very interesting 101in forward-control military machines. The author was lucky enough to take part in that programme, and was amazed to see that even the hard-bitten professional camera crews were genuinely interested in making a comparison between the 1948 and 1976 examples. R.01, for all its bronchial behaviour on that occasion (due to a misbehaving fuel pump), was undoubtedly the star of the Thames TV show.

The 'Millionth' then embarked on a triumphal tour of dealers' showrooms and other exhibitions before being allocated to British Leyland's new Historic Vehicles Collection, where it now lives (and often works for that living) in proud retirement. It must be the freshest and least-used of all the vehicles in that excellent collection.

An interesting sidelight of that ceremony at Solihull (and I regret that I have not been able to find any pictures to prove my point) was that the Land-Rover on the assembly line immediately behind the

(*overleaf*) William Martin-Hurst, Rover's managing director from 1962 to 1969, who was himself responsible for finding the light-alloy vee-8 engine which is now so important to Rover and Land-Rover products. The machine behind him is a 1967 Series IIA 12-seater estate car

'Millionth' had also been placarded, but with a difference. Whereas the 'Millionth' had its own official label provided by Rover publicists, the next vehicle in the line had been marked up by those irrepressible Land-Rover assembly workers: 'Land-Rover No. 1,000,001. Oh No! Here we go again'.

It was a day given over to celebration, ceremony, pomp and circumstance, but it was not long before the work of satisfying many thousands of orders carried on in earnest. Even so, within months a spate of industrial troubles (for which British Leyland was becoming notorious) spread to Land-Rover factories. Production of chassis frames from Garrison Street, in the centre of Birmingham, without which not even incomplete Land-Rovers could be built, was halted for weeks over a complicated labour relations/wages issue, and a whole series of other problems (including a long strike at Lucas, who supplied the Land-Rover's electrical fittings) led to major frustration among the Solihull workforce.

I must also recall, in passing (this episode is covered in more detail in Chapter 10), that British Leyland had encountered a major cash-flow crisis at the end of 1974, and had, effectively, become nationalised by mid-1975. All the car-producing factories in the British Leyland combine had been grouped together as Leyland Cars, and Solihull became merely a 'large car' site in that group.

None of this harmed the Land-Rover's reputation, or prospects, in the slightest, and after three years, during which available capital was spent on more critical projects, it was finally announced that the much-rumoured Land-Rover/Range Rover expansion programme would be going ahead. The master plan was only gradually made public, as work proceeded, but it soon became clear that there were two main intentions. One, quite simply, was to allow many more of the familiar machines to be built and sold. The other, at first intriguing and later exciting to all Land-Rover enthusiasts, was that a progressive updating and modernisation of the thirty-year-old design was intended to take place.

That this process was already 'on paper' in some detail was clear from the company's own internal naming of the V8 Land-Rover, which made its bow, for export only, in the spring of 1979. To Land-Rover Limited staff, this machine was always known as 'Stage 1', and was the obvious first fruit of work then being carried out at Solihull and Acocks Green. Stage II and Stage III, in fact, were never given public names, though it now seems fairly clear that these were the titles for projects as various as the coil-spring suspension Land-Rovers launched in 1983 and 1984, and for the redesigned four-cylinder engines. The early 1980s was an exciting time for Land-Rover Limited.

Every Land-Rover enthusiast with red blood in his veins had been designing his own personal V8-powered version since Rover announced that they were to take over manufacture of the light-alloy vee-8 engine from General Motors. That announcement was made in 1965, the Range Rover was launched in 1970, and the 101in forward-control military prototype followed in 1972, but the public marriage of Land-Rover chassis engineering and V8 power had to wait until 1979.

Although it is always easier to talk about making such changes than it actually is to engineer the job (as those private owners who built their own hybrids had already found out), Tom Barton admits that his biggest problem was in getting approval to go ahead in the first place. Having secured this, it was the unit's bulk which posed the only serious problem. Barton explained:

As I have made clear on previous occasions, we produced the six-cylinder Land-Rover back in the 1960s as a smoother and more refined machine than the four-cylinder versions, but it was not really much faster than the others.

For quite some time after that, we kept on getting feedback from overseas territories, particularly from Australia, where it was obvious that the 60mph cruising speed of the Land-Rover wasn't really enough to match the 80mph speeds some of the Japanese competition could achieve, so when the time came it was obvious that we should try to combine the vee-8 engine with the existing chassis.

It was not quite as simple as it sounds. If the 3,528cc engine in Range Rover tune (which means a unit producing 135bhp (DIN) at 4,750rpm) had been specified, it would have endowed the Land-Rover with a top speed of around 100mph—more than the market required, more than the braking system would cope with, and not at all match-able with the sort of handling and ride which the existing machine provided. For a start, therefore (and I think it is only fair to describe the Stage I machine as just that—a start), a considerable de-tune was needed. In Land-Rover form the big engine produces a mere 91bhp (DIN) at 3,500rpm (which compares with 86bhp at 4,500rpm for the six-cylinder machine), which in itself is not a startling increase. The increase in torque—from 132lb ft at 1,500rpm to no less than 166lb ft at 2,000rpm—is also accompanied by significantly higher overall gearing. For the first time ever since the Land-Rover was announced in 1948, there is a change of axle ratios—from the original 4.7 : 1 to 3.54 : 1—in the same cases.

This much increased torque, incidentally, has made a complete gearbox change imperative, so in place of the normal Land-Rover gearbox, there is the bigger, stronger and more sophisticated gearbox and transfer gearing of the Range Rover, which of course incorporates a central differential, and permanent four-wheel drive.

Chassis and body changes are limited wherever possible. To accommodate the greater bulk of the wide vee-8 engine, and the central transmission, there are changes in the cab. The engine, relatively speaking, is farther forward than on 'conventional' Land-Rovers, and this together with the need for a bigger radiator has meant that new frontal styling (with almost a flush grille) has been adopted.

So much is obvious. The fact that almost all of the other mechanical engineering is unchanged—wheels, tyres, brakes, suspension and related details—is far less obvious as these features are hidden from view. The point is made that the axles themselves were substantially strengthened some years ago, and were used in the forward-control machines without any major problems being uncovered. As with the six-cylinder version, the V8 Land-Rover will only be available in 109in wheelbase form.

In regard to transmission options, and the philosophy governing them, the Land-Rover is now at an interesting point. Way back in the late 1940s the first Land-Rovers had permanent four-wheel drive and a freewheel in the front drive line, but before long this was altered to the still-familiar layout where rear-wheel drive is normal unless the driver takes positive action, and four-wheel drive is automatically engaged when low range is selected. On the Range Rover, and now by definition on the V8-powered Land-Rover, the transmission is in permanent four-wheel drive, in high or low range, and incorporates a centre torque-splitting differential. Tom Barton has gone on record as preferring the permanent four-wheel drive solution for any brand-new gearbox he would be allowed to design, but he also admits that this would be considerably more costly (in tooling as well as in unit costs) than the classic layout. In this choice, as with so many others in the motor industry, the pros and cons must be very carefully balanced.

Why were none of the oft-suggested chassis changes made to this new type—such as coil spring suspension of the Range Rover type, self-levelling, better brakes and other details? Barton comments:

In a word—time and the legislation burden, which I can't expect customers who are pleading for new models to understand. It is fair to say that I could almost keep my design staff occupied in modifying and checking over the design, merely to keep abreast of the regulations which appear and disappear throughout the world.

One point, made with some feeling, was over the question of noise regulations. Not only do these vary from country to country, but the Land-Rover is classified as a truck in some territories and as a private car in others. In any case, the fact that it is sold with knobbly-pattern tyres, and with a generous ground clearance, helps make all noise limits more of a problem than they would be with a private car. Barton comments again:

There's too much space for the noise to bounce around under a Land-Rover. If we put Land-Rover engines into a private car the results are immediately acceptable. Those noise limits, more than anything else, are making us take a new look at the whole question of diesel engine design.

Tom Barton obviously has a lot more that he would like his engineers to tackle, but knows that the sheer practical limits of time, product planning, and available investment will make much of this impossible. He, like Gordon Bashford, is a great sketcher, and loves to talk Land-Rover with anyone sharing his enthusiasms. It is an instructive experience to sit around a table with him, toss outlandish suggestions into the discussion, and await a reaction. First there is a short silence, then, probably, a twitch at the corner of his mouth, and a tight, secret, little smile, and finally a comment which often begins: 'Well, we actually tried that once, you know . . ."

You find it almost impossible to produce any suggestion not already considered by the Land-Rover design team. Coil spring suspension? Tried years ago, and prototypes built ('But a huge amount of investment is involved, because you simply can't—or shouldn't—convert existing frames . . .')—the results stored away for future use.

Larger and more powerful engines? 'Well we *could*. On paper there's a bit more capacity to come, by boring *and* by stroking, though we never actually designed the engine with stretch. But if we changed it, you should *see* the mountain of legislation which we'd have to tackle.'

New body style or methods of construction? 'No problem—after all the Range Rover is very different from the Land-Rover—but our customers like it the way it is, and we offer so many versions that the cost of completely reshaping every one doesn't bear thinking about.'

The suggestion of building simple two-wheel drive Land-Rovers received short shrift from anyone I have talked to at Land-Rover Limited. Quite clearly, the customers do not want Land-Rovers without the option of four-wheel drive. In any case, I am assured, it would not be a simple matter to convert the existing transmission to such a layout. You do not merely disconnect the front propeller shaft, and by the time changes are made to accommodate this the cost savings have nearly disappeared. The alternative of using a Rover private car gearbox without high and low ranges is seen as even less popular still.

In the 1950s, when Stirling Moss and Denis Jenkinson were contracted to drive in the Mille Miglia for Mercedes-Benz, they made several suggestions for improving their race cars, and on each occasion they were met with the solemn assurance that: 'We tried this, and the result was . . .' The same sort of thoroughness seems to pervade the engineering departments at Solihull.

I head this chapter 'Now, on to the second million . . .', and wonder how many readers think I am being facetious. I am not. The more I know of Land-Rovers, and the more I hear of their achievements, and of the management team which continues to develop them, the easier is it to contemplate a date for the second million being completed. On present trends this will be in the 1990s, and I hope I am still around to see it happen.

6 Land-Rover in Battledress

This is certainly not the time or the place for jokes about Land-Rovers being built like tanks. Tanks are fighting vehicles, whereas military Land-Rovers operate behind the front line. Tanks have only one purpose of life—to inflict damage on property and other forces, but a Land-Rover can, within reason, turn its wheels to almost anything. A Land-Rover, in short, is probably the most versatile of all machines on active service today.

No modern fighting force is completely equipped without an integrated fleet of small 4×4s, which can be used for carrying personnel, stores or vital communications equipment, on the highway or across country, which must have the performance to get into and out of trouble spots in a hurry, or which can be used to ferry top-rank officers over terrain completely unsuitable for conventional cars. Specially-adapted Land-Rovers are ideal for this job, as British and other forces have proved. Here at home, throughout NATO, in Commonwealth countries and in fact, all over the world, there are many thousands of Land-Rovers in battledress. No other 4×4, except perhaps the Willys Jeep, is so popular.

Records show that the first three Land-Rovers—pilot-built models —were supplied to the British Fighting Vehicles Development Establishment in 1947, but the British military interest in 4×4s goes back years before that. The Willys Jeep (and there is no point in trying to hide this fact), the world's first quantity-production 4×4, went into production in 1941–2, and was almost immediately supplied on a lease-lend basis to the British military forces. By 1943, with more and more American formations flooding into Britain preparatory to making the invasion of Europe, Jeeps seemed to be everywhere, and their virtues became apparent.

In 1943 the British military authorities decided that they needed a British design of 4×4 to replace their Jeeps. Even if such a machine was not ready before the war was over, it was argued, it would still provide useful employment, and represent a healthy saving in dollars. As I have already pointed out, too, the original Jeep was rather small—in payload and in capacity—and it was thought that

109in military Land-Rovers on patrol with the British forces, and towing a 105mm gun. Although military machines might *look* standard, a great deal of special equipment is sometimes specified

this new 4 × 4 could be rather larger. In the event it was only the relative failure of this project which made quantity sales of Rover-designed machines a possibility.

A group of motor industry companies were called in for consultations, and invited to submit designs to the FVDE, on the basis that although the new vehicle should only be assembled in one factory it could have major components from other concerns in its make-up. There would be one chosen contractor for assembly, to whom other firms might supply engines, transmissions, and axles.

That idea, effectively, was a non-starter, as any civil servant or military adviser with a scrap of industrial experience might have realised. Not even in time of war did competing firms get together like this—not, that is, in the 1940s—and it would be fair to say that no member of the British motor industry was happy to back such a scheme. Rover, for their part, were never invited to become involved, as they were still too small and too specialised. Even after the war, when Solihull needed work to fill it, Spencer Wilks was not interested, as the volumes proposed for this machine, which was unique to the British Army, were too restricted.

Series II 88in military Land-Rover leading a convoy comprising a Humber 'Pig' personnel carrier, and two Bedford transports. Another Land-Rover brings up the rear

After a long delay, during which time the Normandy landings had taken place, a contract was placed with Nuffield Mechanisations Ltd, and by mid-1945 their first prototype had been knocked together, powered by the flat-four Morris engine dreamed up by Alec Issigonis for his post-war 'Mosquito' (later 'Minor') small car. The prototype was rather smaller than its sponsors had intended, and would need a lot of development to become acceptable to them.

Project FV1800 (FV = Fighting Vehicle) was redesigned by Nuffield, but took so long to be finalised that it was not even revealed publicly until June 1950, and was eventually put into production by BMC after the Austin-Nuffield merger of 1951–2. At the end of 1952 civil versions were announced (which indicates that the volume of military sales was insufficient to keep BMC's accountants happy). By this time, however, the Land-Rover was *the* standard by which all other 4 × 4s were measured, and it had already been delivered to the British forces in some numbers.

Considering that FV1800 and Land-Rover both set out to provide the same capability—a nominal 5cwt payload with optional four-wheel drive—they were mechanically very different. Although FV1800 had a marginally longer wheelbase (84in compared with 80in) it was considerably heavier at nearly 3,500lb unladen, and it was mechanically complex.

In complexity, indeed, it was completely different from the Land-Rover. Its basis was a cruciform chassis design, and there was four-wheel independent suspension with chassis-mounted front and rear differentials. In military form it was powered by the B40 2.8-litre Rolls-Royce four-cylinder engine (the six-cylinder FB60 relative, in much-modified form, was later seen in the BMC-built Vanden Plas Princess R saloon car), which was obviously very costly—the Austin A90-powered civil alternative cost £350 less!

A special five-speed all-synchromesh gearbox (five speeds, incidentally, were also available in reverse) was in unit with the front-mounted engine, and a propeller shaft led directly to the rear differential. Front-wheel (i.e. four-wheel) drive was optional, and was achieved by the strange method of connecting front and rear differentials by a pro-peller shaft running the length of the chassis, inside the cruciform.

Although the FV1800 (or Austin Champ, as it was known in civilian markets) was compact at only 12ft long, it was bulky, thirsty, expensive, and not at all flawless over soft ground in spite of its large available wheel movements. It was also incredibly spartan in concept, being made in only one version—open, with canvas hood and sidescreens.

The FV1800 went into use with the British forces at a time when their philosophy was changing fast, in that they were beginning to turn to more general purpose vehicles, thus the specialised FV1800 was not likely to be kept in production for long. Their original large contract, placed with BMC, was for a fixed number of vehicles, which explains why the civilian versions were on offer soon after the military machine went into service.

The Land-Rover, first tried in prototype form in 1947, and first ordered (tentatively—the total order was for fifty vehicles) in 1949, was the absolute antithesis of the FV1800 approach, and the Army were delighted with it. Before long it became clear that the Land-Rover fulfilled almost all the requirements covered by the FV1800, that it could tackle others not thought of at first, that it provided a great deal more operational flexibility, that it was simple and rugged, that it was much cheaper to procure, and that it was instantly available in a great many forms.

For a few years FV1800s and Land-Rovers co-existed side by side in the British forces, even though orders for Land-Rovers soon out-

One of the special-bodied lightweight '½-ton' 88in Land-Rovers now produced for military use all over the world. This was an original version, registered in 1968, with headlamps on each side of the grille. From 1971 the headlamps and side/flash units have been mounted above the wheel arches

stripped the FV1800 contract. Perhaps surprisingly, in view of the almost total lack of protective bodywork on FV1800s, these special 4 × 4s tended to be used as 'high mobility' combat vehicles, up near the sharp end of a skirmish, whereas Land-Rovers were usually employed on a multitude of other tasks in support, and in the lines of communications.

The Land-Rover's versatility was first battle-proved in Korea, between 1950 and 1952, when it was realised that a modern Army wanted more than a British-type Jeep (which the FV1800 really was) with four seats, little weather protection, and no alternatives. Land-Rovers, for their part, could be used for almost any task, whether for carrying people, arms, general supplies, radio and radar equipment, or, perhaps all these at once. They could not, it is true, be used as armoured vehicles—not, that is, in standard form—but even by then private firms were busily working on this sort of conversion.

The '½-ton' military Land-Rover, stripped out ready for air-lifting. The rest of the bodywork, weather protection and equipment is packaged for reassembly after delivery

As year followed year, the military forces found more and more uses for their Land-Rovers, and were delighted to see the steady expansion in power, options and carrying space which Rover could provide. The Land-Rover's original 5cwt payload had been the same as that of the Jeep, and had never been enough, even in civil form. Nevertheless, the British Army confused things considerably by calling its Land-Rovers '¼-ton' models, which referred to the payload which could be carried *behind* the front-seat passengers.

With the demise of the FV1800 in the mid-1950s (though these machines remained on active service for a few years after that) the Land-Rover could, at last and without political embarrassment, be granted its rightful title of the Army's standard ¼-ton 4×4 'Forward Area' vehicle. A generation later, and with no prospect of any rival to oust it in the future, it retains that proud position. Not even in the wide-open world of NATO and the EEC is there a European product to match it. In Italy, it is true, Fiat make the Campagnola 4×4 vehicle, which is quite obviously subsidised by military orders, as it has an expensively tooled body shell (in steel—when will the makers of 4×4s learn about the anti-corrosion advantages of using light-alloy panelling?), and is sold at a competitive price, but is built only in small quantities. The Land-Rover is now the most familiar *and* the most numerous of all vehicles found in the British armed forces—only the well-loved 3-ton Bedford trucks can even approach their record.

Over the years, the British forces, mirrored by customers from Commonwealth and other friendly nations, have evolved two distinct types of requirements for their light 4 × 4s. On the one hand they found more and more uses for a lightweight 4 × 4, of minimum size and bulk commensurate with unbreakable qualities and carrying capacity, and on the other hand they needed larger more rugged machines which still contrived to use a great deal of the same chassis engineering.

The heavier military Land-Rovers evolved from the 107in and 109in long-wheelbase vehicles which had first been made available in 1954 and 1956 respectively. Not only did the forces habitually load their Land-Rovers up to, and beyond, the 15cwt payload limits, but they demanded more and yet more from them. One illustration of this was that they began to use their 109in Land-Rovers to tow light guns, which was itself not a difficult task, but when this was combined with using the full payload of the Land-Rover at the same time it was clear that the ensemble was being overloaded. It was usage like this which led to the development of the '1 ton' Land-Rovers of the late 1960s, and to the eventual adoption of Salisbury axles. All manner of detail improvements—in spring rates, damper settings, and other chassis fittings—have connections with the demands placed on earlier Land-Rovers by the military forces.

The 109in machines, almost always in petrol-engined form (four-cylinder or six-cylinder) find themselves doing any job the forces can think of, from ambulance duties to providing mobile radio/communications stations, from gun and generator towing to small stores delivery duties, from ferrying top-rank officers around the battlefield to delivering the post and the rations, acting as equipment racks (mobile) or even as 'Black Marias' for the Military Police. It is nothing unusual to see dark-blue Land-Rovers fussing around the flight deck of a Navy aircraft carrier, to see a light-blue vehicle pirouetting around the wingtips of Harriers or Jaguars at an RAF base, or to see glossy open versions in khaki, complete with regimental badges, helping the Colonel to take the salute at an Army passing-out parade.

The question of engine preference is interesting, and almost entirely logical. In the first place, customers have to decide whether they want their Land-Rovers to fit in with the fuel usage pattern of their other vehicles (which, in terms of heavier trucks, transporters, personnel carriers or tanks usually means diesel fuel), or whether they want them to be as efficient and cost-effective as possible.

It is a fact that the vast majority of all British and NATO Land-Rovers have petrol engines, though recent large orders have redressed this balance somewhat. There are several reasons for this. Diesel engines, almost by definition, tend to be less powerful than their petrol-powdered equivalents, and the Land-Rover's diesel engine is no exception to this rule. It is also considerably heavier than the petrol engine. This means that performance with a diesel engine is less than with a petrol-powered version, and that where the maximum all-up weight does not change there is an unavoidable loss in useful payload capacity.

Diesel-powered Land-Rovers are more costly, and only begin to pay for themselves over high mileages (which the forces tend not to clock up), though the other side of the coin is that their lack of high-tension spark apparatus is sometimes useful where proximity to explosive materials and atmospheres might be involved. It is worth noting, too, at this point that NATO's search for a universal type of multi-fuel engine (which would give them considerable operational flexibility) has not made much progress at this end of the market, being confined to really expensive diesel (or, more correctly, compression-ignition) engines with high power outputs.

There is absolutely no truth in the suggestion, by the way, that diesel engines are disliked because they are too noisy. Opposing forces have such sophisticated listening devices that any sort of engine noise is picked up at great range, and when one considers the fact that Land-Rovers tend to be operated in concert with big diesel-powered personnel carriers the suggestion becomes truly ludicrous.

For more than a decade now the standard 88in military Land-Rover has looked, and effectively has been, considerably different from the civilian vehicle. Whereas the 109in military Land-Rovers, apart from their 24-volt electrics (if fitted) and some special options, look very much like those in use on your neighbouring farm, the smaller versions are entirely special. They have a unique body, much simpler and less well equipped than the civilian 88in Land-Rover, but are still recognisably from the same stable.

The story of this fascinating '$\frac{1}{2}$-ton' vehicle goes back many years, and originated in the 1930s when military commanders decided that they liked the idea of close tactical air support, and wanted transport

A mighty Wessex helicopter hoisting a $\frac{1}{2}$-ton military machine to its next job. In this stripped-down form it weighs 2,660lb

One way of delivering a military Land-Rover is to drop it by parachute. Here a specially packaged example, complete with shock absorbing landing platform, leaves a C130 Hercules transport plane 'by the back door'

which could be dropped by parachute from the bigger transport planes then being developed. Then, and even during World War II when technological pressures intensified, prototypes were built but were not successful. Even the ubiquitous Jeeps suffered badly in parachute drops, principally because 'chutes were usually too small to ensure suitably leisurely landing speeds, and after the end of the war the pressure to develop such devices were reduced.

The requirement (military forces have a quaint way of specifying a 'requirement' before they even know if such things are practical or even feasible) was for a lightweight purpose-built machine which could be air-dropped, or at least air-transported, to a battleground, and then could be used across country. Only the existing Land-Rover looked like satisfying such a stiff definition, but even when dropped from cargo planes it had to be mounted on sturdy shock absorbing platforms, and there were still many instances during trials of chassis damage occurring after heavy landing.

It was only when the modern generation of large helicopters began to appear that an alternative form of air transportation became possible. Rather than having to drop heavy loads and small vehicles by parachute (and, among other things, risking them falling in the wrong places) it was now possible for them to be placed, softly and accurately, where required. The Westland Wessex (an American Sikorski design built under licence in this country) finally made a lightweight 4 × 4 practical, and the search for such a machine began.

Even thought the Wessex was lusty and versatile, it was thought that it could only carry an external payload, on a sling of about 2,500lb, so this was the target set. It was a very difficult challenge, as witnessed by the fact that a conventional 88in Series IIA Land-Rover of the day weighed at least 2,950lb, and a 109in model no less than 3,300lb. Other manufacturers including BMC were also invited to have a go at this requirement, but the Gipsy was even heavier than the Land-Rover, the Mini-Moke was far too small, slow, low, and only had front-wheel drive. BMC's prototype Austin Ant (which was to the 1100 as the Mini-Moke was to the Mini, but also had four-wheel drive) showed promise, but was not yet in production, did not look like being very rugged across country, and suffered the major handicap of poor ground clearance. It looked as if the Land-Rover would walk away with the new contract, if only the vehicle could be brought down to the weight limit.

But such a reduction—more than 400lb from the civilian 88in machine—was simply out of the question. There were practical limits to the amount of kit which could be discarded, and weight could not be pared from engine, transmission, axle, suspension and rolling chassis at all. It was a stalemate which no one could solve, and therefore it looked as if the air-transportable dream would have to abandoned yet again.

A good old British compromise, as so often in the past, saved the day once again. The RAF decided that the very latest Wessex helicopters with slightly reduced internal payload *might* be persuaded to carry rather more than that terribly difficult 2,500lb target, while

Solihull's designers decided that with a lot of really ruthless redesign *and the ability to provide demountable body sections* they might begin to approach that target.

A completely revised, and very simple body, was provided for a virtually unmodified 88in rolling chassis, one with even less form and even less refinement than the original vehicles of 1948. It was arranged for all the top hamper, the screen, the doors, the wings, the rear bodywork and the seats to be dismantled quickly and easily. Thus denuded of its bodywork the new device weighed in at 2,660lb—just 160lb more than the RAF had originally said was their limit. The stripped body panels, it was decided, could follow on with the next helicopter, and in any case it was stressed that the new model was completely operational, if stark, in stripped-down condition.

Thus it was that the military's new '½-ton' model was born in 1966, and deliveries of this new 'Rover 1', as it is known in the British forces, began in 1968. Bodies, when completely fitted, are every bit as practical as those of the obsolete 'Rover 10' (88in Series II/Series IIA Land-Rover to you or I), and are incredibly simple to repair or reshape.

Only ordered by the British Army, and now out of production, the 101in forward-control Land-Rover used Range Rover engine and central transmission in a special chassis layout

Performance is virtually the same as that of civilian Land-Rovers, for Rover 1 is the same height, and has the same chassis, though its simple body makes it several inches narrower at 5ft 0in instead of 5ft 6in for the more familiar bodywork.

It is worth noting that so far there have been two visually different versions of this '½-ton' vehicle. Up to 1971 these were built with head-lamps in the central grille panel, allied to side lamps and indicators on the rudimentary front wings. Since then, however, a restyle means that headlamps, side lamps and indicators are all now grouped on the nose of modified front wings, ahead of the wheels, and this has been done for the same reason as the civilian Land-Rovers were modified, to bring them into line with legislative requirements for public road use.

This lightweight Land-Rover was such an immediate success that it was rapidly adopted as the standard 88in military model, and has long since displaced the normal-looking 88in models from the ranks. Rover's own sales leaflet points out that Land-Rovers are now 'in military or para-military forces of some 140 territories overseas', and they list the following as its potential roles:

Personnel/load carriers
Command vehicles for artillery/infantry/other arms
Recovery vehicles
Emergency two-stretcher carriers
Light support vehicle towing
Specialist trailer towing, including generators
Signals communications/radio relay
Mobile mechanical/electrical workshops
MT stores/spares
Airfield maintenance/aircraft servicing
Police/civil defence command
Communications/recconnaissance
Fire service vehicles

It can, of course, be fitted with 12-volt or 24-volt electrics. No wonder that a stroll around the delivery parks at Solihull show evidence of a great proportion of these angular but strangely attractive 88in models being made. Distinct and different shades of khaki indicate simultaneous deliveries to several countries, and closer inspection shows a great variety of special optional equipment.

In Britain '½-ton' models have been in use for so long that well-used examples are now regularly sold off at military auctions, and are

Rear view of the forward-control 101in military Land-Rover showing the enormous ground clearance, and the towing hook which could be replaced by a special power take-off for the powered trailer developed alongside it

finding favour in civilian hands. The Army sell off their vehicles when complicated financial calculations show they would be better advised to buy new ones, but this does not mean their useful life is over. These machines will soon be as familiar in private hands as the conventional Land-Rovers, and I have no doubt that the ability to be stripped down will be a great boon to some users.

Finally, in this chapter, I turn my attention to one of the most fascinating hybrids ever to have left the drawing boards of the inventive Land-Rover 4 × 4 designers—the 101in forward-control Land-Rover. This was a very special device indeed, designed at the beginning of the 1970s, announced in 1972, in production only for the British Army between 1975 and 1978, and now withdrawn, probably for ever. It was, and is, so very different from every other Land-Rover built that in my opinion it should not have carried that name, but it upheld each and every one of that vehicle's traditions and abilities.

The need for such a special vehicle arose because the Army found that their 109in military Land-Rovers were becoming progressively more and more overworked. They could be, and often were, overloaded, overstrained and abused, such that the nominal $\frac{3}{4}$-ton payload limit was often cast aside as a triviality. But it was not. Not even Land-Rovers are indestructible, and in the face of reliability problems (and their own cavalier attitude to such limits) the forces formulated a new requirement.

As usual they had to offer this new project to other concerns, but apart from a very promising contender from Volvo in Sweden (the 4140 Series) there was little likelihood of anyone being able to challenge the Land-Rover design team's experience and reputation. The requirement was for a physically larger 4×4 with all the sure-footed cross-country agility of a conventional Land-Rover, able to carry a minimum of 1 ton payload behind the seats, and, equally important, to cope with a 4,000lb towing requirement (across country) for various trailed equipment of which the 105mm Light Gun was tactically the most important.

At first it was thought that a military version of the '1-ton' might do the job, except that this variant of the 109in Land-Rover could not cope with such a payload while towing the 4,000lb Light Gun. Even when fitted with a full-house Rover 3-litre six-cylinder engine and the strongest axles it was not right for the job. Apart from anything else, it rapidly became clear that more loading space and volume was needed, and as the requirement also stated that the vehicle had to weigh no more than 3,500lb (even if stripped down) for helicopter-transported journeys it made adaptation of existing designs impracticable.

When all things were considered, it was obvious that only a forward-control vehicle would be able to do the job. At this point the Fighting Vehicle Engineering Establishment (FVEE) laid down the desired specification (including basic dimensions) and sat back for Rover, or any rival, to meet it.

At the time (this was in 1970 and 1971) a forward-control Land-Rover was in production at Solihull—the revised 110in machine with a choice of engines—but like the $\frac{3}{4}$-ton machine it fell down on payload/towing capacity grounds. Tom Barton's engineers then took a deep breath, and sat down to develop an entirely new forward-control Land-Rover, with nothing else but the Army's requirements in mind. Product planning specialists at Solihull now agree that it was a pity the design went ahead with so little thought to civil possibilities, even though they agree it was in any case a very difficult concept to meet. For what evolved was simply, totally, and exclusively a military tool, making no concessions to styling, or to the creature comforts that civil buyers demand.

Central to the whole design was the need for a whole lot more power and torque. Fortunately, Rover were in the happy position of just putting the Range Rover into series production, which meant that the powerful (135bhp) $3\frac{1}{2}$-litre vee-8 engine, all-synchromesh gearbox, transfer gearbox and centre differential were all available 'off the shelf' without expensive development and capital investment being needed. Indeed, without the existence of this power pack it is most unlikely that the 101in model would have evolved at all.

The Range Rover engine/gearbox/transfer box, therefore, was married to the latest very strong Salisbury axles (with 5.57:1 ratios), and fitted to a solid new chassis frame with 101in wheelbase. Simple half-elliptic spring suspension was chosen (the springs were above the axle tubes, to aid the ground clearance, which was a healthy 10in under those axles), and 1-ton 109in brakes and 9.00–16in tyres completed the basic chassis layout.

The forward-control driving position did nothing for the soldiers' comfort, but certainly allowed provision of a generous (8ft 2in long) load floor, and the engine was located virtually between the seats. As with the successful 'Rover 1' 88in military Land-Rover, most of the 101in machine's bodywork could be removed quickly to aid air-transportation. In stripped-out form it weighed precisely 3,500lb, and this compared with 4,040lb in complete ready-to-fight condition. The more powerful Wessex and (later) Puma helicopters can handle this sort of weight without difficulty.

When it was first shown in public in 1972, one of the main attributes of the purpose-built 101in model was said to be that it could be linked to the new generation of powered trailers to provide an articulated 6×6 combination which should be ideal for cross-country motoring. This was achieved by having a rear power take-off combined with towing hook (a very clever and technically complex engineering and geometrical problem), and was ideally demonstrated when Rubery Owen's powered trailer was hooked up to the rig. However, although the concept worked, and worked very well, military operational requirements changed before quantity production began. Although the 6×6 capability still exists in the 101in Land-Rover, no trailers to use

Not a gimmick, but a serious project, was this private-enterprise Land-Rover armoured car, based on the 109in chassis. Stuart Bladon, now Deputy Editor of *Autocar* magazine, is driving

that ability have ever been manufactured, and in that respect it is a 101in feature which is wasted.

Surprisingly, in view of its agility, and of the Land-Rover's reputation in general, this special forward-control concept has never found great favour in other friendly countries. Between 1974–5 and the end of 1977, never at more than 20 vehicles a week, 1,945 were built, almost all were delivered to the British Army, and production has now ceased. During this time the 101in monopolised a simple but special line at Solihull, and needed more than its fair share of hand work to be assembled. When I asked if it could possibly have been a profitable project in view of the limited sales, I received a guarded response; I got the impression that it had been as important to keep the Army happy as to make a profit out of the contract, and there are still hopes that it, or a development of it, will be revived in due course.

The 101in Land-Rovers have bluff fronts, and look impressive rather than attractive. Brochures list an even more extensive number of duties which they could carry out, and the point is made that they could find civil (at least in government terms) applications. For their

For the Army, there was this forward-control Land-Rover fire engine

size—they are 7ft tall and more than 6ft wide—the 101in machines can be surprisingly nimble. Across country they have a very hard and bumpy ride—those fat springs and big dampers (but no self-levelling) do a very solid job without much concession to driver comfort—while on the road they can be rushed up to about 80mph before the hydraulic tappets of that powerful vee-8 engine pump themselves up and inhibit further progress. Motorists on the M3 in Surrey occasionally receive an invigorating shock when passed by a 101in machine on test from nearby FVEE facilities.

In view of the price of a Range Rover, it is hardly surprising that our cost-conscious military procurement agencies have not found a place for it in their line up. Four-wheel drive vehicles are strictly working vehicles in the modern military system, and a Range Rover is far too good for that sort of job. On the other hand a private car often provides more ideal transport for 'on the road' occasions, which leaves the Range Rover, a luxurious dual-purpose design, rather out in the cold. On the other hand, will a military use evolve for the new Stage I V8-powered Land-Rover? I wonder.

It is worth repeating the Rover statistic which claims more than 140 countries among its customers for military Land-Rovers. On the assumption that this includes only 'friendly', or at least neutral countries, and that certain countries closely linked economically and in military terms to the United States will automatically choose Jeeps, this means that Land-Rovers have been proved successful by almost every government with whom they can possibly do business. Maurice Wilks certainly never thought of his 1947 brain-child as a fighting vehicle, but in many cases it has undoubtedly been just that. In military, as in civil, terms, Land-Rovers have many successful years ahead of them.

7 Behind Closed Doors . . . Designing the Range Rover

The Range Rover is such a popular machine, and has attracted so much praise, that it is difficult to see why it took so long to evolve in the first place. No other 4 × 4 vehicle in the world combines the same virtues and seems to sell to so many different people—yet it is a fact that Rover had little idea of the potential demand when they launched the car in 1970. Like the Land-Rover before it, the Range Rover defined its own market sector, and built solidly on that base in succeeding years.

This is not meant as a criticism of the Rover sales force, or of the product planning staffs. The Range Rover was so different from the Land-Rover in every way that they had no yardstick for comparison. However, it emphasises the Range Rover's unique appeal, something which the competition is only now beginning to understand. For a Range Rover is not just a large and sure-footed workhorse, but a very attractively presented package. In some parts of the world ownership of a new Range Rover brings more prestige (and envy!) than the purchase of a Rolls-Royce or a Cadillac.

A Range Rover is no Land-Rover, and that is not a platitude. Until 1975, indeed, the two machines were completely different. Since then cross-fertilisation of designs (Military 101in and the V8 Land-Rover) has blurred the distinctions. Its price, its specification and its performance place it in an entirely different market from any Land-Rover. The Land-Rover design team, however, are happy to claim it as one of their own, and the tail-gate badging ('Range Rover—by Land-Rover') makes that very clear.

As with many other famous cars, the model finally offered to the public was considerably different from that originally dreamed up by its sponsors. I have to say, however, that the early designs were not as attractive, nor as integrated, as the Range Rover which has now evolved. Nevertheless, the one would not have been possible without the others, and the way in which the evolutionary process developed is interesting to recall.

Although the Range Rover's production design was settled by 1968, first thoughts on a 'big Land-Rover' came as early as 1950 or 1951. There was no product planning department in those days, and all major decisions on new models came down from Maurice Wilks. Usually he would explain his ideas to the sales staff and to his engineers, listen carefully to their own thoughts on the future, and make up his mind from there. It was informal, but it worked. Wilks' 'batting average' was very high throughout the years he was in charge.

Wilks had seen the success of the original Land-Rover, was relieved to see that the P4 saloon cars had been safely launched, and was still in an expansive mood. Without really knowing what he wanted, he thought it necessary to close the gap between the two ranges. Gordon Bashford, who was naturally in at the birth of every new Rover design at the time, recalls that:

> Maurice decided that we now needed (another) new vehicle, still with cross-country capability, that was more suitable for road use, as opposed to the workhorse concept of our Land-Rovers. On that basis I was asked to work up the first layout, or package. At that time it was to be based on P4 components.

The original prototype Range Rover of 1967, as styled and engineered by Spen King and Gordon Bashford. It was a remarkably 'integrated' design for a vehicle shaped by a non-professional

At that time, Rover could not possibly afford to go ahead with an all-new design involving a lot of expensive tooling (though they were willing to consider a new body shell), and as the P4 saloon car was the only current alternative they had to using the Land-Rover chassis, design concentrated on these components.

P4, of course, was the generic name for the range of four-door saloon models conceived just after World War II (the '75' came first in 1949, and the last of all was the '110' built in 1964), cars which were staid, silent, gentle and dignified in the true Wilks manner. Under the skin, however, they had solidly-engineered chassis frames, independent front suspension, and modern engine designs, where the high quality and durability was built in, rather than hastily added on at a later date.

As always happens with new models, there was a great deal of sketching ('the 4B pencil process' as it is sometimes cynically known in the motor industry), and several false starts before any settled sort of design began to appear. As Gordon Bashford told me:

Rear view of the 1967 prototype Range Rover, where differences from the final production machine are more apparent

The prototype Range Rover had a two-piece tail gate and a very useful loading area. The separate tail/stop/flash lamp lenses were only used to get the car on the road in a legal condition, not as a final solution

We messed about, scheming layouts for two- *and* four-wheel drive at first. Even though the P4 chassis was a strictly conventional car component, we could still use standard parts and ingenuity. We went through a whole series of schemes, and I promise you that I also considered front-wheel drive as well!

Maurice Wilks was not at all sure what sort of new product he wanted sold. He could not strike a balance between 'off-road' capability and public highway performance at first, and this meant that the use of four-wheel drive transmission lay in the balance. In fact the original prototype had four-wheel drive, which meant that the chassis had to be much-modified to allow a Land-Rover front axle and leaf-spring suspension to be fitted.

Although Wilks had invented yet another excellent name for the new machine—Road Rover—he had most certainly not invented a stylish body shape. That first car looked ungainly and angular, and a study of the illustration makes its nickname—the 'Greenhouse'—quite obvious. It was, indeed, the last new Rover product that Wilks personally styled (or rather, instructed someone else how to style). He had had all manner of difficulty in adapting his ideas from the sleek and classic shapes of the 1930s to the full-width styles of the 1940s, and would soon appoint David Bache to look after P5 and subsequent models.

Work on the Road Rover went ahead without much haste, but after that original prototype had been built it was decided that a conventional two-wheel drive transmission should be used. This immediately meant that there would be more 'Road' than 'Land' capability in the design, but at the time this was what seemed to be needed. Maurice Wilks first officially notified the Rover directors of this new project in 1952 (although, informally, this sort of work is never kept a secret from any top executive). They gave it tentative approval, as a future production machine, in 1953. Yet it never appeared, was never even committed to production tooling, and died an unpublicised death in March 1958.

Over the years there was a good deal of development and a great deal of change. As the project became more widely known within the company, more and more managers put in their opinions, and the unfortunate result was that the Road Rover seemed to lose some of its purpose. Gordon Bashford's summary, relayed to me in the mid-1970s, tells it all:

> Everybody seemed to like the first car, and after the directors had approved it the vehicle was moved into Dick Oxley's area. This meant that it had become a current project—my department dealt with basic research. Despite Dick's efforts to maintain the original, slab-sided concept on Land-Rover lines, his brief from management escalated. They thought the original was too austere, and asked for changes to the light-alloy body shell, involving the shape and needing complicated pressings, In this way it got bigger, grander, heavier and more costly.

More than this, it was being overtaken by events. While the Road Rover was being developed, a station wagon version of the Land-Rover itself had become available, and was proving to be very popular. In spite of the hard ride and limited performance of this model, it became obvious that it could satisfy most of the potential customers seen as likely to buy a Road Rover.

So that its concept can be compared with that of Range Rover, a

Once the Range Rover project was handed over to Rover's styling department, a full-size clay model was worked up to establish the final production shape. This, in fact, stayed remarkably close to the outlines of the original car. Note that at this point the vehicle is still called 'Road-Rover', that two different grilles are being studied, and that Rover 2000 wheel trims are proposed

look at the final (i.e. 1958, when cancelled) Road Rover specification is instructive.

The basis of the car (for it was really a car, and not a cross-country vehicle) was a modified version of the P4 chassis, though the links were rather tenuous as the wheelbase had been shortened from 111in to 97in and the side members narrowed by $\frac{1}{4}$in (entirely new side members had to be pressed), while laminated torsion bar independent front suspension (P5 type, which was still itself under development) instead of the P4's coil springs was used.

The engine fitted to final prototypes was the 1,997cc Rover 60 four-cylinder unit, then being used in production Land-Rovers, though the entirely new 2,286cc Land-Rover engine which was to be announced in 1958 would certainly have been used when production of the Road Rover began. There was no alternative engine scheduled at first, though Land-Rover experience shows us that demand would surely

This bird's-eye view of a Range Rover chassis in left-hand drive form shows that no space is wasted. In the rear suspension, the mounting of the A-bracket locating member is clear, with the Boge self-levelling strut inside it, and the clever positioning of the dampers (one ahead of, one behind the axle) is obvious. The finished product should be compared with pictures of the original prototype

have forced this through, and as there was sufficient physical 'elbow room' in the chassis for the P4's six-cylinder engines, this provision would not have been difficult.

The transmission was that of the conventional P4 passenger car, with a four-speed manual gearbox (synchromesh on top, third and second gears—one better than the Land-Rover), and an optional over-drive, the P4 hypoid bevel axle with the same ratio as the saloon car, and normal road-pattern tyres. There was no provision for four-wheel drive (the chassis was not at all suitable for such an installation, especially as the independent front suspension would have had to be abandoned), or for an alternative set of ultra-low gear ratios.

In hindsight it seems clear that the Road Rover's principal failings were in a lack of special purpose, and a lack of style. No matter what its sponsors might think, the car was no more and no less than a large and rather ungainly estate car, without cross-country capability, or any of the other special attributes of the Land-Rover.

During the development phase the project had certainly 'lost its way', and nowhere was this more obvious than in the styling. In final form, and inspired by 1950s Chevrolet station wagons, it had a bulbous two-door estate car body shape, with upper and lower tail-gates. All skin panels were in light-alloy pressings, but the main frame of the body was to be pressed steel. The waist line was high, and ran straight through from nose to tail. There was a large grille having some resemblance to that planned for P5, a sharply wrap-round screen, and wrap-round rear corners. It was no longer a greenhouse, but neither was it attractive.

The complete car weighed 2,850lb (not all that much more than a Land-Rover estate car of the period, and considerably lighter than the P4 saloon from which the chassis was derived), was only 13ft 8in long, and no less than 5ft 3in high. Ground clearance was a mere 5.4in, which emphasises that this was in no way meant to be a cross-country machine.

The last surviving Road Rover now seems to have been scrapped, though Dick Oxley of the Rover company ran it for a number of years, finally with a four-cylinder Rover 2000 engine fitted.

For the time being, therefore, that was the end of Rover's involve-ment in larger vehicles of this type. The engineering team was quite small, and capital funding for new projects limited. Once the Road Rover project had been discarded the company was completely wrapped up in the new Rover 2000 project; innovative designers like

Range Rover facia and instrument panel. Of the centre instruments, only the clock was standard at first, though the minor face-lift of January 1973 rectified this. It is now possible to have overdrive on your Range Rover, which means that an additional lever sprouts from the tunnel in the floor

Gordon Bashford and Spen King, too, were also much involved in exciting projects like the gas-turbine cars.

Even so, Peter Wilks (who began to direct all engineering operations in 1964) and Spen King never abandoned their belief that one day the world would be ready for a 'luxury Land-Rover', nor that the company would back them when the time was ripe. Although Land-Rovers continued to sell like hot cakes, competition from firms like Jeep (with the Wagoneer) and Toyota proved that four-wheel drive machines with more performance and better equipment were in demand all over the world.

The chance to start again came in the mid-1960s, at a time when the P6 car was in production, the gas-turbine cars finally abandoned as uneconomic, and before the merger mania hit the industry. As so often happened at Solihull at the time, a new project evolved, rather than was planned, and the principals involved were Spen King and Gordon Bashford; Peter Wilks, with day-to-day responsibilities in all engineering areas, was happy to let them get on with the job.

King and Bashford started again from first principles, thought a lot, argued at length, and made mountains of sketches before actual design began. For its purpose the Land-Rover was fine, but the new machine they had in mind was to be completely different. The Land-Rover was small; the new vehicle would be larger. The Land-Rover was too slow; the new machine would be much faster. The Land-Rover was very durable, but hard on its occupants; the new design would have to be much more civilised. The Land-Rover was stark and purposeful; the new car would have to combine luxury with practicality. It was to be every bit as fast, large, and practical as a Wagoneer, but it would also have to be a Rover. It would have to provide an ingenious amalgam of Land-Rover engineering and Rover private car performance.

Right away, King and Bashford agreed that four-wheel drive was going to be fundamental; leaving it out of the Road Rover had been a mistake. They wanted to keep all the Land-Rover's cross-country abilities, which made high ground clearance, optional ultra-low gear ratios, 'knobbly' tyres, and sheer unbreakable ruggedness essential. On the other hand they thought that the Land-Rover's hard suspension was unacceptable. Spen King wanted to see much more wheel movement available (this has been his design philosophy for a great number of years), a much softer and more car-like ride on sealed surfaces, and more acceptable handling.

Gordon Bashford, who made all the original schemes, now takes up the story:

> We started off in the early 1960s by considering the car with the old six-cylinder P5 3-litre engine. We called it the '100in Station Wagon' because when I had finished sketching up the first design package, the wheelbase turned out to be 99.9in, so I said we should round it up, and call it after that dimension. That was one of the few things we didn't change from first to last. We had no serious competitor in view at that time, because I don't think there was an existing machine which did what we were trying to do.
>
> In order to get a good ride and acceptable performance across country, an awful lot of thought had to go into the suspension design. It was then that we decided that we must have low spring rates, large wheel movements, and good damping. Self-levelling (which we have at the rear) came in at the same time. If you have low rates and long wheel movements with a high payload potential, then levelling is essential.

Design, therefore, commenced at a time when Rover, led by managing director William Martin-Hurst, were agonising over their medium-term future. The question of engines was foremost in this conundrum, mainly because the P4/P5 i.o.e.v. design was becoming distinctly aged, and could not be further developed without losing either its refinement or its reliability.

Although there is no doubt that the new '100in Station Wagon' could have been a fine design with the best of the 3-litre 'sixes' installed, it would inevitably have lacked the vital spark which, in the event, did so much for its prospects. That spark, of course, was the lusty $3\frac{1}{2}$-litre vee-8 engine which is now such an important 'building block' in the Jaguar-Rover-Triumph design scene.

The story of how William Martin-Hurst found, negotiated for, and eventually secured, the light-alloy vee-8 engine has been told in great detail many times. It is enough to repeat that Martin-Hurst first studied the General Motors engine design when on a business visit to Mercury Marine in North America in 1963, found that GM had just decided to take it out of production (on cost, not engineering, grounds), approached GM for a licence to take over manufacture, and eventually succeeded, making the agreement public in 1965. Martin-Hurst recalls incredulously that he had a great deal of difficulty in convincing GM that he (and Rover) were serious in taking over what, to them, was an obsolete design.

The attraction of this ex-Buick $3\frac{1}{2}$-litre vee-8 to Rover was that it was potentially very powerful (even in standard form it was more powerful than any existing Rover engine), that it was compact and already proven, and that it was very light. Cylinder blocks and heads, together with other important castings, were all light-alloy, and more than 200lb were saved compared with the old straight six unit. In bulk, the vee-8 was virtually no shorter than the six, and considerably wider, but this was not considered a drawback when the potential of the design was considered.

It is worth recalling why General Motors dropped the design in the first place. It had been new (if recognisably developed from another GM 'cast iron' engine) in 1960, although experimental work had originated in Detroit back in 1950, and was only forced out in 1963 when an alternative unit with thin wall cast iron materials became available for the second generation of GM compact cars. Technically, GM had no complaints, and the engine was proving to be very reliable, but the production engineers in Detroit were anxious to return to simple and cheap cast iron components once they proved to be as light, and rather cheaper, than the light alloy parts in this engine.

The complete early-production standard Range Rover rolling chassis

What was a disadvantage to GM was a positive boon to Rover. For one thing, they would be taking over an already-proven vee-8 engine design (something which might occupy more than five years of their own designers' time, even if they had got it right first time around), and for another they knew that the alternative thin wall cast iron techniques were not yet available in Great Britain. Work on converting the design to British production methods, and on preparing the engine for use in most future Rover models, began at once. The vee-8 engine, still built in its original $3\frac{1}{2}$-litre form, is now the most important single power unit in production at Rover.

King and Bashford accepted its potential joyfully for their new project, which they still knew only as the '100in Station Wagon'. Later, briefly, it would be known as 'Road Rover', and it only became Range Rover when the styling had been settled and the project approved. Considerable redesign was needed, not least to the new transmission (to take account of potential power boosts which the engine might have in future years), but the engine itself slotted comfortably into the engine bay originally laid out with the six-cylinder 3-litre unit in mind. By the end of 1966 it was time to begin building the original prototype.

The kernel of the design was the transmission, which was quite different from that of the Land-Rover. In a marketing somersault which has never properly been explained to the author, it was decided to give a car, which would spend *less* of its time off the road, *more* traction. The new vehicle was to be endowed with permanent four-wheel drive.

To take care of transmission wind-up between front and rear, and after considering the status of the new vehicle, a third differential was added to a system which was basically like that of the Land-Rover. Behind the new four-speed all-synchromesh box was a two-speed transfer box, allied to the centre (Salisbury) differential with limited-slip mechanism, and a locking device. There were no limited slip mechanisms in either of the axle differentials.

This familiar proving shot demonstrates the remarkable range of wheel movement which gives the Range Rover such a soft and comfortable ride in most conditions

Also central to the whole concept was the long-travel suspension. Live axles were retained at front and rear, and both were suspended on vertical coil springs, controlled by telescopic dampers. Spring rates were low, and damping firm, while available wheel movement was between 8in and 9in. To make sure that all the available rear suspension movement was useful, whether the vehicle was empty or fully loaded, a self-levelling Boge Hydromat strut was fixed between the chassis frame and the axle casing. This was self-powered, pumping itself back to a pre-set length due to suspension movements, and had been discovered quite by accident when Spen King and Gordon Bashford had been touring accessory stands at a Frankfurt motor show.

The rest of the concept, technically speaking, was just as interesting. Four-wheel disc brakes, with twin-spot front calipers, split hydraulic circuits, and a separate transmission handbrake, were a feature, and suspension location was ensured by radius arms, a Panhard rod at the front and an A-bracket at the rear. Safety belts were to be built into the front seats (instead of being fixed to the floor of the body) and there would be provision for power-assisted steering even though it was not proposed to offer it at first.

All this was substantially settled in 1966, but there remained the problem of the body and its style. Normally this would present no problem, as David Bache's styling department had already built up a fine reputation, both inside and outside the company, and there is no doubt that he would have relished the job of tackling such an all-new project. The problem, in this case, was not about ability, but about time.

In 1966 Rover's styling department was hard-pressed. They were dealing with all manner of advanced private car projects (like the shaping of the 'fast-back' coupé Alvis, based on the Rover 2000 base unit, and the studies which were to lead to the massive P8 Rover 'flagship' which never actually got into production) and could not spare time to look at a new cross-country vehicle.

Spen King, therefore, with a considerable reputation as an 'amateur' stylist already to his credit, gained permission to have a go at the styling and layout of the new machine himself. He had, after all, been responsible for the rear-engined T3 gas-turbine car, and for the splendidly individual mid-engined P6BS sports coupé, which was still being built at that moment. Not without help, on an informal basis, from styling engineers, Spen King and Gordon Bashford set to and designed a wonderfully practical and chunky two-door station wagon

shape for their new chassis. Unlike the original brief for the 1947 Land-Rover, there was a considerable capital allocation to be gained for body tooling, so the shell was a stylish, complete, and—of its type —shapely composite of pressed-steel and pressed light alloy. In certain ways it was quite obviously a prototype, and one which would need to be changed. The wheels were unadorned, the grille as simple as could decently be used to screen the radiator, and some standard Lucas lamps were used for side/tail/stop illumination. In all other ways, however, it was an astonishingly practical machine, which instantly won the hearts of management when they saw it in near-finished form.

While the prototype '100in Station Wagon' was being built, however, Rover's management had changed. Having themselves taken over Alvis in 1965, they had looked long and hard at the future cost of new model capital expenditure, been appalled by its implications, and looked round for a partner. In the winter of 1966–7 they joined forces with Leyland Motors, who at once became the dominant partners. The problem for the new project was not whether Rover's own management would like it, but whether the new paymasters—Leyland— would approve as well.

Front seat safety belts are mounted direct to the seats themselves, which accordingly are massively strong on their own account. When tipped forward they also slide forward, to ease access to the rear seats

8 Range Rover —
Another World-wide Success Story

For a moment it is now worth reviewing the industrial situation which crystallised immediately after the Leyland–Rover merger of early 1967. The new group instantly took up third place in the private car league table (behind BMC and Ford), and in money terms it was easily the largest producer of commercial vehicles, with AEC, Albion, Leyland, Scammell, Standard, Alvis—and Land-Rover now owned by the same concern. Even before Sir Donald Stokes, Leyland's chief executive, began to think about the last merger, the biggest of all, with BMC, he had time to work rapidly through the future plans presented to him for study by Rover's management.

Millions of unkind words have been written about Leyland's methods in recent years, but they showed nothing but logic in their appraisal of the Rover–Alvis situation. Of all the new ideas offered to them by existing management, they speedily gave the go-ahead to the introduction of the vee-8 engine, they pushed on with development of a new large saloon (the P8), and they were positively ecstatic over prospects for the Range Rover. Cancellation of the mid-engined P6BS/P9 sports coupé was a sad blow to Rover enthusiasts, but few shed a tear over the demise of the fast-back Alvis coupé.

Right from the start, Sir Donald Stokes and his Leyland colleagues made it clear that they were delighted with the Range Rover project. It was big, it was practical, it was modern, and it promised to be supremely versatile. In every way it looked likely to be as successful as the Land-Rover had become. On the other hand no one, least of all Rover's sales force, *really* knew how successful it could be, how many they should aim to sell, and how they should price the new machine.

Leyland agreed, but they also authorised its development for production. They wanted it quickly—space to assemble it could be found in one corner of the South Block where P4s had once been erected—but they also wanted a more professionally presented vehicle than the prototype which had still not been completed by Spen King's team. David Bache's styling team was therefore called in.

Range Rover interiors are a clever mixture of the luxurious and the practical. You *could* fold down the back seat and carry a pig or two behind, but most owners use their Range Rovers for private car and leisure activities

Starting from the basis of the King–Bashford prototype, the styling engineers built up new mock-ups—$\frac{1}{4}$-scale and eventually full scale—in clay. In spite of full investigations, and a complete development programme, it is true that the finalised product put up to management for approval was virtually the same basic shape as that original. One illustration in this book shows the full-scale mock-up at an intermediate stage, when it was still badged as a 'Road-Rover'.

New details which had evolved included the chunky and very appropriate side/tail/indicator lamp clusters, the recessed panel feature along the body sides and the internal hingeing of the doors. On the other hand, the petrol filler cap was hidden behind a flap, a different type of door handle was proposed, Rover 2000 wheels were fitted, the rear quarter opening window profile was not yet settled, the ventilator extraction, and the front and rear detail styles still showed alternatives. All of which goes to show the care, and the great detail, with which major styling jobs were tackled.

At one time it was hoped that Range Rover production could begin

The Range Rover in 1970 production form, with the two-piece tail-gate open. Initial owner experience suggested that some sort of non-slip surface was needed on the loading floor (so that gun dogs, for instance, could keep their footing when jumping aboard) and this has now been added to the specification

in 1969, or at least in the winter of 1969–70, but neither date proved practical. At one stage, certainly, the company were so certain of an early start-up that they considered having a team of Range Rovers entered in the *Daily Mirror*'s London–Mexico World Cup Rally, which was due to start in April 1970. The scheme had to be dropped, and they were replaced by the much less exciting Austin Maxis. Even so, Leyland (British Leyland by the time final go-ahead was given) were so anxious to get the Range Rover on sale that the final stages of development had to be rushed. This is not to say that the first production vehicles were deficient in any way—the company's experience was that the Range Rover immediately established its own reputation for strength and durability, just as the Land-Rover had done—but that the final touches normally made to trim and decoration items had to be cut out.

In particular, the standard of trim and interior finish was not what some of the company's management would have liked. Tony Poole of the styling staff told me some time ago:

The trim and what we call the soft furnishings are always settled last, and ideally we would have liked another year to get the right balance between appearance, function, and cost.

While the Range Rover was under development, British Leyland looked on it as an ideal candidate for export to the United States, where Rover's sales were small. That, however, was in 1967 and 1968. After that the impact of burgeoning anti-emission and safety legislation bore down heavily on the Range Rover's prospects. It was designed with United States sales in mind, and would sail through all the crash test and other safety requirements imposed by that sometimes short-sighted nation. The problem was that Range Rover production volume would be low in the foreseeable future, that changes required purely for the United States market would be extensive and costly, and that British Leyland management did not think it worth pursuing the matter further. In particular, the problem of 'de-toxing' the big vee-8 engine was thought to be serious. That apart, it is interesting (if fruitless) to consider how the Range Rover would have fared in the wide open spaces of the North American continent, and how it would have stood up against the mighty competition of Willys, fighting from the strength of its home ground.

Gearing up for production of the Range Rover was a major undertaking, as no component was shared with the existing Land-Rover range, and only the engine was already an established major component. The frame itself came from an outside supplier, as did some body shell panels, along with the springs, dampers, self-levelling strut and some axle components. Rover, for their part, had to find space alongside the busy Land-Rover assembly tracks to assemble the vehicles, and—more important —they had to find somewhere to machine and assemble the bulky transmissions.

Major factory expansion in the Birmingham area had already taken place in the mid-1960s, which allowed certain component assembly operations to be shifted out of Solihull. Happily, British Leyland were also able to take over an ex-CWS Ltd factory next door to the old Tyseley building, which logically enough became known as Tyseley No 2. A comprehensive reshuffle of facilities and operations meant that Range Rover transmission components could be machined in existing company factories—casings and bell housings were made at Tyburn Road, Erdington, for instance, and gearbox machining and assembly takes place at Tyseley and Acocks Green. Although space for expansion existed at the Cardiff factory, 4 × 4 transmission work was not, nor

In the hustle and bustle of Solihull's final assembly shop, this is the climactic point which every visitor wants to see—where the body is lowered carefully on to the chassis by slings

ever has been, centred on that site, which concentrates on the building of transmissions for Rover and Triumph private cars.

It is fair to say that within months of its formation, British Leyland was under pressure to start showing results, and particularly to introduce new models. The most important of all new models under development was the Morris Marina, which had been started by BMC before the merger. Originally it had been hoped to have this ready by 1970, but when it was delayed, and in the face of a blank year for new model launches, British Leyland urged both the Triumph Stag and the Range Rover forward to premature release. The Range Rover actually made its bow in mid-June 1970, but was acknowledged as being reserved initially for home market sales only, and it was also said that deliveries would not begin until September. Very few, indeed, had reached their eager customers' hands before the Earls Court Motor Show in October, and the first price rise (of no less than £232, or nearly 12 per cent) came at the beginning of 1971.

As with the Land-Rover in 1948, so with the Range Rover of 1970 and 1971: the production build-up was slow. In North American terms, management and workforce were on a 'learning curve' for several months, making sure that the complex new machine fitted satisfactorily together, and that it performed as it should. One of the problems was a scarcity of vee-8 engines, but the major one was in getting the product right. Only eighty-six production cars were delivered from Solihull by the end of August 1970, and in the next 12 months a further 2,537 followed. By the end of the 1970–71 financial year the rate of production was rising towards 100 Range Rovers a week—a mere drop in the ocean compared with the demand which had developed—but at the start of that period it was a good week which showed more than twenty or thirty vehicles rolling off the new assembly track.

One technical change, in fact, was needed after only the first few months, and took effect in the winter of 1970–71. All prototype Range Rovers had a limited-slip feature in their centre differential, and the vehicle went into production like that, but within months it was deleted from the specification. Although it brought a considerable cost saving to the design, the limited-slip feature was discarded because it was not thought to contribute much to the Range Rover's effectiveness across country. Because it had permanent four-wheel drive, the Range Rover's traction had always been impressive. The half-way locked feature was thought to be of marginal importance, and it was accordingly dropped.

There is no doubt that some members of the management team were very worried about the Range Rover's prospects. Even when priced at a mere £1,998 in Great Britain—a price which looks ludicrously low compared with the levels since achieved (in 1985 Range Rover prices start at £13,632)—they thought it might deter the customers, particularly when compared with the price of 109in Land-Rovers which started (in basic form) from £948. It is worth noting that at the time—June 1970—a Rover 3500 (the P6-based car) cost £1,944, the big 3½-litre Rover P5 saloon cost £2,343, and a 4.2-litre Jaguar XJ6 sold for £2,606 if you could get hold of one.

The problem was that no one at Rover could forecast the Range Rover's future. They had a good idea that it would find a multitude of 'gentlemanly' tasks which had hitherto had to be tackled by Land-Rovers, that it would rapidly become the 'in' vehicle for towing horse boxes, that it would soon become the ideal 'estate' car (for gentlemen who still had estates), but they could have had no idea of its instant popularity.

Everyone, it seemed, could think up a desperate need to own a Range

Rover. Everyone, whether they lived in the depths of the country, or in the centre of a city, could find a use for a Range Rover. It was not until the first road tests were published (and the implications of 15mpg fuel consumption sank in) that their ardour cooled a little. Even so, the Range Rover looked ideal for the big organisations who found Land-Rovers a bit small and a lot too slow. Range Rovers for recovery tasks (AA, RAC and the commercial organisations), and for police motorway patrol duties were ideal.

The Press received the Range Rover with acclamation, not least because many of them were ready to receive any good news from the beleagured British Leyland empire. They thought it was smart, practical, technically clever, and definitely trendy. Certainly they agreed with Rover's own advertising claims for the Range Rover when it was launched:

> There are four basic types of car in the world. And you can own all of them. A luxury car. A performance car. An estate car. A cross-country car.

One might argue over Rover's choice of the four basic types (no sports cars? no economy cars?), but it was easy to agree with their contention that the Range Rover was all of them. There were oblique references to Jensen's unique four-wheel drive FF coupé ('There's permanent four-wheel drive, usually only found on £7,000 cars . . .'), and a lot of advertising copy which suggested that the company viewed their new model as a car rather than as a working machine.

In all the descriptions, all the fine opinion-forming words, and all the driving impressions published, one potential drawback to the Range Rover was usually missed. Unlike the Land-Rover, whose bodywork has proved to be virtually indestructible, the Range Rover body shell was built up on an inner skin of steel panelling, and only the skin panels were in light alloy. This meant that, unavoidably, while a Range Rover was built to 'last for ever' (as many Land-Rovers appear capable of doing), many early models now show this evidence of the use of pressed-steel panels by rusting in a very non-Land-Rover manner; this was realised, and extensive anti-corrosion treatment has been applied to the bodywork since that time. Range Rovers, of course, were built around a massively

One of the Range Rovers which eventually bridged the Darien Gap edging carefully down the lightweight ladders which, incidentally, were needed more than 400 times on this tremendously difficult journey completed in 1972

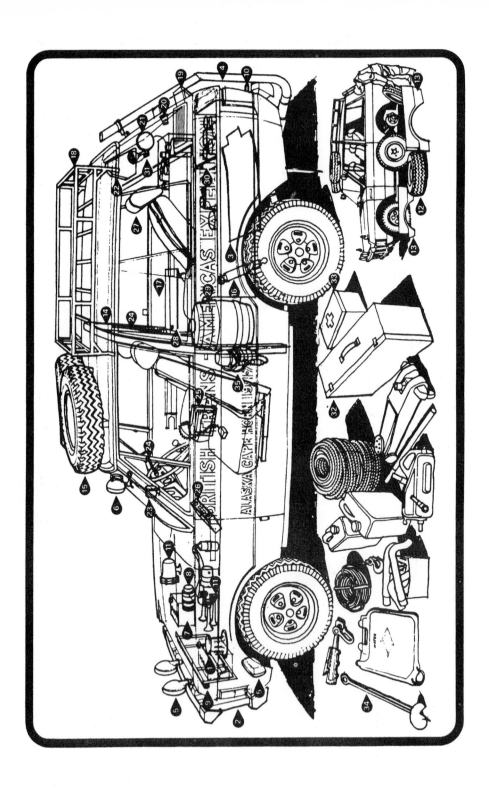

strong and rigid chassis frame which would soon give them a fine reputation for rugged behaviour.

Range Rovers at first sat uneasily in the no man's land between private car use, and working vehicle status. Their four-wheel drive system allied to chunky all-condition tyres proclaimed their willingness to tackle any sort of going. Their styling and equipment, on the other hand, seemed to say that here was another fine car in Rover's traditions. From the very beginning it seemed certain that Range Rovers would not be used very often as load carriers, at least not in the basic sense. One could visualise a Range Rover carrying dogs, and perhaps sacks of provisions or other dry goods, but it was hard to see any owner loading pigs in the back, carrying trussed calves in a sack, or moving a load of gravel from one site to another. The Range Rover, in short, was altogether too respectable, too valuable, too middle-class, to demean itself in that way. Rover's own researches had shown that 75 per cent of Land-Rover owners used them at one time or another for leisure purposes, but found them slow and unsuited for long-distance work; the Range Rover set out to solve this problem for them.

It was not so much the styling, or the mechanical ability of the new model which was so exciting, but the performance. Rover's own engineers claimed a maximum speed of 96mph, but *Motor* in their independent test of January 1971 recorded an astonishing 99mph. This was so much faster than the Land-Rover's abilities (only the six-cylinder series IIA

(*opposite*)
The Darien Gap Range Rovers carried an enormous amount of extra kit, as evidenced by this ghost view of one of the machines ready for the attempt. Among many other things, this included a coffee maker and a built-in safe! Key: **1** Front mounted capstan winch 3,000lb capacity; **2** Reinforced bumper/cow catcher guard; **3** Petrol tank undershield; **4** Raised exhaust extension; **5** Four quartz-iodine spot and fog lights; **6** Two swivel spot lights; **7** Split charge two battery system; **8** Heavy duty alternator; **9** Radiator muff; **10** Four extra towing eyes; **11** Sirens and air horns; **12** Swamp tyres; **13** Removable wing panels; **14** Roll-bar; **15** Roof mounted spare wheels; **16** Special low-temperature shock absorbers; **17** Insulated body panels; **18** Roof rack; **19** Steps on tailgate; **20** Power point in rear of vehicle for cooker etc.; **21** Heated rear screen; **22** Wiper/washer equipment for rear screen; **23** Extra instruments—tachometer, oil pressure and temperature gauges, ammeter for split charge system; **24** Map reading and interior lights; **25** Two-way vehicle radio; **26** Stereo-tape player and radio; **27** Reclining seat with full safety harness and headrest; **28** Built-in safe; **29** Water keg; **30** Partitioned stowage lockers; **31** Inspection light, 26ft lead; **32** Fully comprehensive tool kit; **33** Medical supplies; **34** Extra equipment, hand winches, ground anchors, cable, tow ropes etc.; **35** Coffee maker

model of the day could creep past 70mph—the others were all limited to maximum speeds in the 60s) as to put it in an entirely new market sector, and it was close enough to that of the company's own Rover 2000 private car as to be a bit embarrassing. In spite of its hefty weight (nearly 3,900lb ready for the road) acceleration was very spritely indeed, and in this respect it could outpace the Rover 2000 in nearly all respects. Fuel consumption, on the other hand, was rather a bad joke because there was no way of avoiding the penalties imposed by a massive and bluff frontal area (a Range Rover was 5ft 10in wide *and* high), by the all-up weight (which could approach 5,000lb when fully loaded), and by the hefty transmission losses. Not even at a steady 30mph would economy rise above 25mpg, at 70mph this was down to about 16 or 17mpg, and it was possible, with enthusiastic use of the throttle pedal, to record figures as poor as 12mpg.

Not that this mattered. Driving a Range Rover was such enormous fun. The ride was soft and level, the ambience impressive, the performance adequate for imposing ones will on a normal traffic stream, and the road holding (for such a high and bulky machine) was quite incredible. There was a good deal of body roll, and the steering was relatively heavy at low speeds, but in general to drive a Range Rover was to enjoy a new motoring experience, if for no other reason than the view from the driving seat. One point about those seats, by the way, was that the seat belts were built into them, which was another Rover 'first' as far as our own motor industry was concerned.

It was not only the Press, and the impatient mass of customers, who were impressed by the Range Rover. At the 1970 Earls Court Motor Show it was awarded a Coachwork Gold Medal by the IBCAM judging panel, beating no less a car than the Triumph 2.5PI Estate in its £1,000–£1,750 Utility class. The same match would be staged in 1971, with the same result—another Gold Medal for the Range Rover. After that the company decided to rest on their laurels, let others battle for the crown, and declined to enter in future years.

The question of who would buy Range Rovers was soon answered by the statistics—not those for whom the advanced specification was originally intended. One of my favourite whimsical motoring writers, Michael Scarlett of *Autocar*, summed up the Range Rover in his 1971 Motor Show review as follows:

Much as we continue to delight in the Range Rover, there is a slightly wistful feeling at the back of our minds that we couldn't really find enough use for it. And that there is a clique of town people who buy those very functional beasts for unfunctional reasons. The Range Rover seems to have become, to some extent, Surbiton Man's suburban safari car— giving him that get-away-from-it-all expedition feeling as he commutes to the station.

It was all very true. At this stage one was far more likely to see a Range Rover disgorging a load of children at the school gates, loading up that bulky antique piece of furniture in the local high street, or being used as a mobile grandstand at the local sports day, than doing anything more useful on farm or estate than towing a horse box or caravan. For a year, at least, it was *the* trendy new car to have, and in 1971 it was only overtaken by the new vee-12 Jaguar E-Type in this sort of prestige stakes. It was quite astonishing as to the number of respectable professional men who found that they had actively needed a Range Rover for years, but had not been able to satisfy that need. Country doctors found them ideal for their practice; farmers with any social pretensions at all discovered how different the word 'Range' was from the word 'Land', and how necessary it was to have one of these big new 4 × 4s; vets could always make an excuse for all that loading space; motor racing teams were easily converted to the idea of prestige linked to a lot of space *and* self-levelling into the bargain (for towing their cars); and any tradesman with a need to carry goods and impress his customers found a Range Rover essential. In short, the new model was everything Maurice Wilks had perhaps intended for his Road Rover of the 1950s, and it was everything *plus* traction which the biggest and best estate cars had been offering for some years.

By the time the purchase pattern had shaken down—which is to say by the time exports had begun in some volume, and by the time the trendies had fluttered away, wraith-like, to some new candidate for their approbation—it became clear that the vast majority of sales were to customers with a real need for dual-purpose transport. Most were from businesses involving construction or a considerable degree of travel over unmade and perhaps slippery surfaces, to farmers, estate managers, builders, tradesmen connected with off-road travel and delivery, and to a whole variety of customers with a need for hefty towing jobs where the Range Rover's weight and carrying capacity would be welcome.

Rover's own researches, indeed, showed that nearly three-quarters of all Range Rovers were sold where there was a towing requirement—for horse boxes, trailers, caravans, car recovery, car delivery, glider towing, boat transport—and that requirement was linked to an ability to get going and keep going across unfavourable terrain. If the Land-Rover had been other than a long-term success, the news that Range Rover sales were eating into those of the older design might have been a shock, but in the event this was something of a relief to the company. Although the Land-Rovers being displaced were the more expensive (and more profitable) six-cylinder versions, usually in station wagon form, it was a fact that the Range Rover was potentially even more profitable, and it was also true that indirectly this allowed a few more Land-Rovers to be built.

Not only was the vehicle fast and impressive, but it was also undoubtedly very solid and safe. The RAC were themselves so impressed that in 1971 they awarded the Dewar Trophy to the company (jointly with Peter Wilks, the company's technical director at the time of the Range Rover's development) in a citation worded 'for outstanding tech-

The Queen's Range Rover has a unique back seat arrangement with four seats which can be folded up, and support bars all around the periphery

nical achievement in the automobile field'. Don, the British brake materials manufacturing company, had already awarded their 1970 Don Safety Trophy to the Range Rover (having withheld it in 1969 after no new model had reached the high standards set by Jaguar's XJ6 in 1968).

All this was very satisfying to the company, and to the customers who were still waiting impatiently for their own orders to be fulfilled, but stylist David Bache was most proud of the fact that the Range Rover was chosen for exhibition in the Louvre, in Paris, as an 'outstanding example of modern sculpture'. This, to Bache, was the ultimate accolade for a design which had always been hemmed in by a large number of practical constraints, and indirectly it was a salute to Spen King and Gordon Bashford who had conceived the design in the first place.

As with British Leyland's Jaguar XJ6, so with the Range Rover, initial comments pointed out the vehicles' phenomenal value, second thoughts suggested that prices had been set too low, and third remarks were that it was high time these prices were jacked up to equalise the products with the huge demand for them. At first, certainly, the Range Rover was offered at a startlingly low price, by almost any standard. During 1970, when sold in Britain at a mere £1,998 (how low that price appears today!), it compared with £1,786 for the Land-Rover six-cylinder station wagon, and with £1,878 for the big Volvo 145S estate car. Jeep's Wagoneer, which might have been considered a competitor, was not sold in Britain, though road tests had been published in the specialist magazines.

With Range Rover prices passing through the £9,000 barrier during 1978 (and that, mark you, is a figure for the basic car, even without desirable extras like the Fairey winch already described), it seems clear that its low price was not allowed to persist for long. It would be wrong, however, to suggest that Range Rover price levels amount to profiteering, because unhappily the general level of prices in Britain has also soared in the intervening eight years.

The company points out that the basic specification of the Range Rover may not have changed, but that the general detail and equipment of the vehicle has continuously been improved. The last (Land-Rover Limited) management also claim that the new model was introduced with little more than a 'best guess' idea of what it would really cost to produce, and that it was only marginally profitable at first. That sort of thing is often done with new models to allow them to become established.

Between June 1970 and the end of 1978, the general level of car prices in Britain increased by about 400 per cent, or 363 per cent if different levels of taxation are taken into account. Therefore, I thought it would be valuable to prepare a table of Range Rover prices, current at each anniversary of the vehicle's announcement. Since June 1970, when the Range Rover was launched, its selling price in Britain has soared by more than 500 per cent, 458 per cent including tax, without killing the demand. The following table shows the way the price movement has taken place:

Range Rover prices

Date	British Basic Price (£)	British Total Price (£)*
June 1970	1,529	1,998
June 1971	1,706	2,230
June 1972	1,881	2,274
June 1973	2,025	2,413
June 1974	2,842	3,387
June 1975	3,689	4,316
June 1976	4,638	5,426
June 1977	6,396	7,483
June 1978	7,289	8,528
December 1978	7,821	9,151

*Total prices include taxes. Between 1970 and March 1973 purchase tax (at various rates) was applied to the basic ex-factory price. Since March 1973 this has been replaced by (a) Special car tax, at 10 per cent of ex-factory price, and (b) by VAT, variously levied at 10 or 8 per cent.

At the end of 1978 the total taxation 'take' was 17 per cent, compared with 31 per cent in 1970.

Yet, for all the price inflation, and the fact that in relative terms a Range Rover costs 25 per cent more than it did on announcement (compared with other British cars), there is still an enormous demand from all over the world. Recently, I asked my local Jaguar–Rover–Triumph dealer how long it would take for a Range Rover to be delivered. The sales director smiled politely, said he would be delighted to take and process my order, hoped I would not be wanting any outlandish extras, and said that he *hoped* I would get my Range Rover inside a year, perhaps in nine months.

Production built up at Solihull just as fast as space, facilities and expertise could be assembled. The single assembly track was always full to capacity—there was no space for any duplication, and any sugges-

Built on one of the very first production machines is this long-wheelbase three-axle high performance fire engine, by Carmichael of Worcester

tion of substituting Range Rover capacity for any of the hard-pressed Land-Rover lines was met with ferocious resistance from the sales force. The 10,000th Range Rover (which sounds a puny achievement compared with the enormous sales of Land-Rovers) was built at the end of 1972 after a very slow build-up, the 20,000th followed in the spring of 1974, and the first really significant achievement—50,000 Range Rovers—was notched up in mid-1977. For the past few years the theoretical capacity of that single assembly track has been 300 Range Rovers a week, though the figure of 250 is nearer the mark in a week with minor shortages and problems. This, of course, is achieved with single-shift working, and with the maximum possible supply of vee-8 engines from Acocks Green, where the machinery also has to supply engines for the Rover 3500 private car, the Land-Rover Ninety and One-Ten, and sports cars like the TVR and the Morgan Plus 8. *That's* variety.

Range Rovers have now been in production for more than fifteen years, and still there are no important variations on the basic theme. This is simply and solely because demand for the original version could not, and still cannot, be satisfied. 'What would be the point,' Jack Reardan (Land-Rover Limited's sales director) told me, 'in offering other versions when it would mean less Range Rovers being available altogether?' This problem, and others concerning the Range Rover's future, are discussed at greater length in later chapters.

Changes to the original design have been few and far between. Management concern over the hasty release of the original Range Rover, and the fact that deliveries could not begin at once, proved to be unfounded, but the styling department's opinion that more time and thought should have gone into the furnishing and interior equipment proved to be justified. Everyone, Press and customers alike, loved the mechanical layout of the Range Rover, but a good few of them thought that the interior was a little sparse and 'plasticky' for their liking.

Rover replied that, above all, a Range Rover was meant to be a working tool, but they also had to admit that it was being used for more gracious occasions and leisure purposes by many of the buyers. In particular there was comment about the blank spaces left in the instrument layout (for 'extras' to be fitted) and about the quality and type of carpeting. Therefore, in January of 1973, it came as no surprise to see revised versions put on the market.

Inside the cab, the previously optional instruments were now to be standardised, which is to say that four minor dials (oil pressure, oil temperature, ammeter and clock) now lived in the centre of the facia, bracketing the face-level ventilation grille. Although hard-wearing plastic material was retained on the footwells, the transmission tunnel was now to be carpeted, and a new non-skid material was fitted to the floor of the loading compartment. This last change, incidentally, had been made in response to two perfectly valid complaints—that objects being carried in the back tended to skate around and hit the sides, rear, and seat backs, causing damage, and that animals (particularly gun dogs, for which the Range Rover was particularly ideal transport) found it difficult to keep their feet when the vehicle was being driven over undulating terrain.

Mechanically, the really important change was that power-assisted steering became available. During 1972 the manual steering ratio had already been lowered to reduce efforts, particularly at low speeds in soft ground. Power-assisted steering which is still an option (the cost is approximately £300 in Britain, including VAT) is very popular, and found on the majority of Range Rovers produced. Almost as valuable, if not mechanically essential, was the rear window wipe-wash feature which was to be standardised. The shape of the Range Rover had always meant that its back window soon became obliterated with filth thrown up by the road, and sucked in by aerodynamic currents. These changes, incidentally, coincided with a price increase from £1,984 to £2,025 (basic), which was considered very reasonable by those able to assess the improvements made.

Since then, and apart from the extras already described, the Range Rover has been built in basically the same specification for more than six years. A minor change to the high-range step-down ratio has been made, which affects gearing only marginally, and to keep abreast of the changing EEC exhaust emission regulations the engine has had to be recalibrated, with a nominal power loss of 5 bhp which does not seem to have affected the performance at all.

Once the initial batch of cars for the British market had been delivered, exports began in earnest, and before long the Range Rover was attracting orders from all over the world. The North Americans, who might have appreciated owning Range Rovers instead of Cherokees and Blazers, were denied that pleasure because the car has not been cleared through the mass of rules and regulations protecting the North American motor industry. Customers in wide-open territories (like the Middle East and Australia) came to appreciate the much higher performance of the Range Rover compared with existing Land-Rovers or, indeed, compared with any other true dual-purpose 4 × 4s, and anyone with even a scrap of latent snobbery in his make-up hurried to take over a Range Rover so that his neighbours' Land-Rovers would instantly look old-fashioned. By 1975, two-thirds of all Range Rover production had been exported. In recent years the preponderance of export deliveries has increased even more. In the two financial years 1975–6 and 1976–7, four out of every five Range Rovers were sent overseas, and only 4,000 stayed in Britain. There is no doubt that every vehicle built could find a customer in an export market, and even then the waiting lists would persist.

Twice in a generation Rover have introduced a 4 × 4 which was a world-wide success from the day it was announced. Twice they have been in the very satisfactory position of witnessing a seemingly endless demand for their products. But in the next few years big changes are promised. Whereas 4 × 4 production was stifled by factory limitations for years, by 1985 it was possible to make many more than before. When world 4 x 4 demand, in general, rises again in several overseas territories, the latest Land-Rovers will find many new customers.

Why should this be? In the case of the Range Rover, *Autocar*, who carried out a thorough comparative test and survey of 4 × 4 models in 1978, had this to say:

What we really set out to determine is whether the Range Rover is still worth its ever more formidable price—now well on the way to £9,000. It has changed very little since the original introduction eight years ago; but it now costs four times as much, and there are many more competitors on the market. Does it still come out on top?

Quite simply the answer is that it does in every way—including, alas, price. The tougher the conditions, the more the Range Rover will show its superiority over the others. The rougher the going, the more one will appreciate the competence of its suspension design. The steeper the hill, the better able it is to show off its low ratio prowess, and—here's an important point—the happier the driver is that he's going up what seems to be a vertical wall in the Range Rover and not anything else. Finally, show it an ordinary road or a motorway, and the Range Rover becomes a rather large but extremely fast and competent car.

Need any more be said?

9 Range Rover —
if Money were no Object . . .

If you ask any group of motoring enthusiasts to name their ideal fleet of cars, and they were reassured that money was no object, I could almost guarantee a response. Almost all of them would name a Ferrari, a Porsche, or a Lamborghini as necessary to flatter their egos, and all of them would name a Range Rover as the all-can-do back-up.

This is not supposition. I have seen straw polls like this, even organised, or participated, in a few myself, and there are never any surprises. The choice of trendy supercars tends to change from time to time, but a Range Rover is the cornerstone of everyone's planning. It is not that a Range Rover is so desirable, or so trendy and fashionable anymore; it is just that, to so many people, it is essential.

That said, it is usually fascinating to hear what follows. How many times have I sat in on such discussions, and heard snatches of conversation like this:

'Yes, but its a pity the Range Rover only has two side doors. I'd like four, and I'd be willing to pay for them . . .'

'The gearbox is a bit heavy and a bit chunky. Why don't they make them with automatic transmission? Or wouldn't it work . . ?'

'I need the space of a Range Rover, but I'm not sure I really need the permanent four-wheel drive. I'd like a two-wheel drive type . . .'

In the face of this, and in the face of the demand for Range Rovers, it is not at all surprising that a thriving specialist industry has arisen to supply all manner of special modifications for these fine machines. If not bodywork modifications, then engine tuning. If not automatic transmissions, then overdrives. If not simply lily-gilding, then complete reworking. It would be easy to assume that the factory wanted nothing to do with such things, nor that they ever took an interest in them. It would also be quite wrong.

If you ask any Range Rover enthusiast what he really thinks should be done, you will get predictable response—four doors and/or longer wheelbases, two-wheel drive options, and an automatic transmission option to the manual arrangement. I am betraying no secrets when I say that the factory has already investigated all these features, that prototypes have been built (and, in some cases, are in constant use), and that one or more will find its way into production in the 1980s.

But not yet. The problem, put to me so succinctly, and on separate occasions by Mike Hodgkinson, Tom Barton, Jack Reardan, and Roland Maturi (who, as the chief product planner, *really* knows all about market trends), is one of capacity. With Range Rover demand running so far ahead of Land-Rover Limited's capacity to produce and deliver, it would be madness to spend a great deal of tooling capital on additional features which—almost by definition—would make it more difficult, not easier, to build the maximum number of Range Rovers on one assembly line. No one argues that a bigger, more diverse, range would be desirable. Within reason, everyone is agreed as to how this should be done.

'The most insistent demand we identify,' Maturi told me, 'is for Range Rovers with automatic transmission, and for four-door versions. By that, incidentally, I really mean five-door versions, except that the Range Rover's tail-gate really isn't a door as it opens in two pieces. It would be quite possible to accommodate a four-door version of the shell on the same 100in wheelbase, but *ideally* it would be preferable to offer a four-door vehicle on a long-wheelbase chassis.'

Suddenly, therefore, we are beginning to talk in big-money terms. Not only would very substantial body modifications be involved (and at a production rate, now, of 250 a week, with 500 a week talked of for the early 1980s, I need hardly say that body shell tooling is of a fairly comprehensive and expensive nature), but a new chassis frame would be needed, along with a redeveloped rear suspension, rear transmission, and many other details. A longer Range Rover, too, would be unavoid-ably heavier. Land-Rover Limited would not want to sell the larger version with less performance than the original, so it presupposes that more power would have to be extracted from the vee-8 engine. Now does the company's reluctance to take such a large step look more logical?

They are more sympathetic to considerations of an automatic trans-mission version. There is nothing wrong with the Range Rover's existing four-speed all-synchromesh gearbox, but it is best described as sturdy and utilitarian. In addition, many of the markets to which (restricted) supplies of Range Rovers are available find manual transmissions some-thing of antiquities. In the Middle East, for instance, where one gains almost as much 'face' by owning one's own Range Rover as by having a Cadillac or a large Mercedes, almost every car in this price class comes with automatic transmission, power steering, air-conditioning, and other up-market private car goodies.

This ambulance conversion on the lengthened Range Rover base was engineered by Spencer Abbott (Engineers) Ltd, and would probably give its unfortunate occupants a better ride than any other cross-country recovery vehicle

Automatic mates well with the Range Rover philosophy. The engine itself produces lots of lusty low-speed torque, which is the sort of delivery on which the average automatic transmission thrives, and the sort of speed and transmission speed fluctuations involved in loose-surface motoring are easily soaked up by such a flexible transmission. There would be no insuperable installation problem—a torque converter and the usual Borg Warner Type 65 box would fit neatly in place of existing Range Rover manual transmission—and it would mate logically enough with the transfer box and central differential which is presently fitted to all Range Rovers. There is evidence to suggest that in marginal conditions an automatic Range Rover would perform slightly better than a manual version, owing to the way the torque converter always slips slightly, and it could cushion any harsh effects on driven wheels which might be on the point of breaking loose from the road surface. The bad news, though, is that the already rather poor fuel consumption would suffer slightly, and in some conditions I have little doubt that nothing better than 12 or even 11mpg would result.

The question of ideal transmissions, or what the customer might prefer, is something sure to bring on embarrassment and a certain amount of subject-changing when discussed with Land-Rover Limited management. Careful perusal of letters to motoring magazines for the past eight years makes it quite clear that many, many people have been complaining that two-wheel drive is not offered, though I have to say that most of these correspondents do not appear to have owned a Range Rover, nor have the funds with which to consider one. On the other hand, as I have already stressed, it is a fact that the Range Rover offers more traction as standard than a Land-Rover does (you have to make a positive decision to engage four-wheel drive on a Land-Rover, on the Range Rover it is always provided), yet it is used much less often off sealed tracks and surfaces.

Tom Barton makes no bones about his thoughts on the matter:

> The Range Rover was always designed to provide permanent four-wheel drive, and the best possible system at that. I simply don't agree that a two-wheel drive model is preferable—and I can tell you that it would be complicated and expensive to provide such a variant.

It would not, for instance, simply be enough to disconnect the front propeller shaft, for this would merely allow the centre differential to wind itself up into an overheated frenzy, and the vehicle would get nowhere. Even if a way were found of locking the drive to the (disconnected) front axle, this would still bring the centre differential into operation on a permanent basis, a function for which it is not designed.

The only solution, Barton points out, would be to disconnect the transfer box arrangement and centre differential assemblies, and discard them completely, while at the same time changing the live front axle for a new and simple forged axle beam. This would leave the original Range Rover four-speed gearbox in place by itself, needing a new tail cover, through which drive to the back axle could only be arranged by a severe crank to the unavoidably offset differential. Personally, the author would then be tempted to suggest using the Rover 3500/Triumph TR7 five-speed gearbox instead, which is already matched in machining terms to the vee-8 engine, and which would then provide a built-in overdrive fifth gear which suits a Range Rover so well. But the fact remains that the company does not agree that two-wheel drive versions should be offered, and maintains stoutly that they cannot see the demand for them:

'After all,' Tom Barton quipped, 'a two-wheel drive Range Rover would offer no more traction than a private car of the same weight, and there would then be no real reason for buying one. You might as well buy a Transit van and have it customised!' Somehow, though, I do not think he was serious.

The company is equally adamant that cheaper and simpler Range Rovers are not the way for them to expand a range if there is an opportunity. Roland Maturi acknowledges that there is a sizeable price and marketing gap between the more expensive Land-Rovers and the Range Rover, but thinks that this gap is best filled by improvements to the Land-Rover rather than by degrading the Range Rover. The Range Rover, he points out, has a good deal of social *cachet* among its customers, particularly in certain overseas markets, which he does not want to see destroyed. 'Many people have discovered that the quickest way to destroy a "prestige" image is to offer a cheaper version that doesn't have as much. Unless, that is, you start by announcing the most simple vehicle first, which is what we did so long ago with the Land-Rover.'

Most Range Rover customers, on the contrary, seem to want to add exclusivity and optional equipment to their Range Rovers, and although the choice of extra equipment from the factory is not so wide as it is for the long-running Land-Rover, there are several good ways of making a splendid machine even better.

The company finds that full air-conditioning is more and more in demand, and already offers a choice of systems. The most popular fitting (added after the Range Rover has been built) is fitted in the dash area, where a condenser is housed in front of the radiator. There is an alternative roof-mounted unit, now only offered in very special cases, particularly where the ambient temperature is so high that the area in front of the radiator must be left uncluttered.

Having proved a market for an overdrive on the Land-Rover since 1974, a Fairey two-speed overdrive (primarily for the home market) has been approved for the Range Rover since the beginning of 1978. This assembly, built entirely by Fairey in their West Country factory, bolts on to the tail of the conventional gearbox/transfer box assemblies, and (with suitable juggling) can be arranged to provide no less than sixteen

forward gears and four reverse gears in all. This astonishing total is arrived at as follows. The conventional box has four forward speeds and one reverse. The transfer box has high range and low range, which doubles the possibilities. The overdrive is a simple two-speed cluster—offering direct drive as normal, or a 28 per cent gearing up if the separate gear lever is operated—which is not epicyclic like a conventional car-type Laycock overdrive, and can therefore be applied to any of the 'normal' eight forward and two reverse gears. Nevertheless, it would be a brave and resourceful man who tried to use all those gears in any form of sequence.

In truth, the overdrive is normally only of practical use for gearing up the high-range transmission in on-the-road use. As road tested, an overdrive-equipped Range Rover is significantly *slower* in overdrive top than in direct top, though fuel consumption at steady speeds is improved by up to 15 per cent throughout the speed range; the faster the Range Rover is going, the more marked is the gain in consumption. In Britain the overdrive costs around £300, but can be fitted in no more than three hours (it has to be done as a conversion, by a dealer, after manufacture). Rough calculations show that up to 60,000 miles trouble-free motoring would be needed to pay back the conversion cost.

When the conversion was announced, Leyland Cars (as they then were) claimed a top speed of more than 110mph, which is quite simply not possible, especially when the cautionary speed limit of around 100mph on Range Rover tyres is considered. Because it also has to be engaged by separate lever, it follows that using the overdrive as a ratio 'splitter' is only possible for a contortionist. Its main selling point, amply proved in practice, is that more relaxed cruising is possible.

Purely for interest, it is instructive to quote the overall ratio possibilities now available on an overdrive-equipped Range Rover:

High range, in overdrive: 3.09, 4.65, 7.56, 12.56
High range: 3.95, 5.95, 9.67, 16.08
Low range, in overdrive: 9.19, 13.84, 22.50, 37.38
Low range: 11.756, 17.69, 28.78, 47.84

(*opposite*) The Smith five-door conversion looks enormously practical, and cleverly uses almost all of the original Range Rover's panels and glass. The wheelbase is no less than 135in

More performance to match the possibilities of the overdrive are not available from the factory. However, if a Range Rover is not to be used where it will take up improbable engine angles the special Range Rover Zenith–Stromberg CD2 carburettors are not required, and—if the customer was feeling particularly sporting and adventuresome—a complete SD1 engine tune, with 9.35:1 compression ratio cylinder heads, SU carburettors, different camshaft, and 155bhp (DIN) at 5,250rpm could be installed. This would be extensive *and* expensive, but it would result in better acceleration. On the other hand, there would not be as much low speed torque as with the standard engine, and the problem of exceeding recommended maximum speeds for the tyres would remain. Road-pattern tyres, incidentally, are available in a size suitable for the Range Rover, but these are definitely not recommended by Land-Rover Limited. Although they are adequate in terms of speed rating and static load capacity, the company do not consider them rugged enough for the uses to which most owners, however careful, seem to put their Range Rovers.

If money really was no object, from 1975 it would have been possible to take a Range Rover to Duncan Hamilton Ltd, of Bagshot in Surrey and have the engine turbocharged. This, the company claimed, boosted the maximum power from 135bhp for the standard engine to 205bhp (at 5,000rpm) for the turbocharged unit. No changes were thought necessary to the transmission (and, at the time, British Leyland said they thought the drive line would be able to cope with the extra torque loadings). The conversion, which had to be done on vehicles already registered, cost £575. This is certain to have increased substantially since then.

Most Range Rover buyers, however, are quite happy with the performance as offered by the factory, but a fair number (with healthy bank balances) have their vehicles 'customised' in one way or another after taking delivery. This is not to say that the standard Range Rover is at all deficient in any way—it is, in truth, as well-equipped, and probably more refined, than any other 4 × 4 in the world—but it reflects the sort of custom, and the sort of prestige possibilities, which are now connected with the machine.

Such customers—they vary from the proverbial rich Arab to the discerning businessman—would rather have the best Range Rover in the world than a Rolls-Royce which is no better nor any different from those of his colleagues. Land-Rover Limited are delighted that this should be so—such publicity can only be good for the vehicle's image—

Wood & Pickett sell several variations on a customised Range Rover theme. This is the Sheer Rover, complete with new nose, wheels, and road-pattern tyres

but are equally convinced that there is no market, in any economic volume, for factory-constructed examples.

They leave this sort of thing to coachbuilding specialists, of whom Wood & Pickett, of West London, are noted exponents. Wood & Pickett were already well known for their superbly modified Minis before they turned to the Range Rover in 1976, and their Park Royal address gives a clue to the fact that they employ craftsmen with many years of experience in the coachbuilding concerns once grouped in that sector of London.

There is no such thing as a 'standard' conversion from this concern, as the work done depends on a customer's requirements and, frankly, the amount of money he has to spend. Their brochure lists at least 100 separate items, embracing restyled front-end arrangements to suspension changes, interior improvements and equipment for expeditions, complete conversion to either four-door or six-wheel (twin rear axle) conversions, with or without lengthened basic wheelbase, alone or in conjunction with each other.

You could, for instance, spend well over £6,000 on a custom-built six-wheel conversion (supplied, I suspect, by Carmichael of Worcester, who have this sort of conversion approved by Land-Rover Limited), or you could merely settle for a completely reworked interior for more than £1,500. The possibilities are, quite literally, endless.

The ultimate expression of a group of modifications on the basic standard 100in two-door body shell is the Sheer Rover ('Sheer' means 'lion' in Iran, where the first examples were sold). The interior of the standard vehicle is completely gutted, and re-equipped with a new facia and instruments, with Recaro reclining front seats, with choice pile carpet on the floor and loading area, with Connolly hides and/or Dralon on the seats, with fully plumbed-in air-conditioning, with Woolfrace cast alloy road wheels, and with an exterior respray to Rolls-Royce standards. To list the items available, or often fitted, would fill several pages; it is enough to say that anything normally found in handsomely coachbuilt cars—cocktail cabinets, sliding sunshine roofs, radio telephones, television installations, complex radio and cassette fittings and reading lamps, for example—are all available. For expedition use you could even be supplied with water purifiers or tents which fix to the body, and a small foldaway motorcycle, to be carried on slings at the rear of the vehicle, is also offered.

The key to many expensively-modified Range Rovers is a lengthened wheelbase. Because the Range Rover has a sturdy and separate chassis frame, this is achieved relatively simply, but it is the body shell changes inescapably linked with the work which take more time (and cost more money). In many cases making the wheelbase longer—at times up to 36in longer—is linked with providing a four-door conversion, or by providing an entirely special type of body and vehicle function.

Carmichael of Worcester have taken this a stage further, by not only manufacturing special long-wheelbase chassis, but also by making twin rear axle models available. In technical terms, this is achieved by leaving the original rear axle in its intended position relative to the centre transmission and to the driving seat, and by mounting a further Range Rover axle and wheels behind it. This is the Carmichael 6 × 4 chassis, which denotes a lengthened wheelbase, but in which the third axle is not driven. These are very suitable, for instance, for crash rescue tenders, due to their speed and increased load-carrying abilities.

The extra axle is not needed to provide sufficient traction, for the Range Rover has an excellent cross-country performance in all conditions, but is essential if the more ambitious 'working' conversions are to be supplied. These may include high-performance fire tenders, personnel carriers, cross-country ambulances, or applications where lighter-than-standard wheel loading is required. Although the front half of the standard chassis frame is retained by Carmichael in building up their six-wheel conversions, the back half of the frame is effectively new. The 'kick-up' over the axles is longer, differently shaped, and the members have to be more sturdy to look after the heavier and differently concentrated suspension stresses.

It is a much more straightforward task to lengthen the existing frame, so that a four-door body shell may be erected, and is often achieved merely by cutting, then lengthening with new inserts and reinforcing members along the main side pressings, all in the best vintage-style engineering technique. Range Rovers modified in such a manner come from various sources, and are usually distinguished one from another by the shape and method by which the extra pair of doors is incorporated.

In almost every case, the standard body shell is cut in half (the practical—and obvious—transverse cut line is immediately behind the line of the door closing pillar), the two sections are moved apart by the increase in the wheelbase, after which new doors, floor, roof and suitable filler panels are fabricated to complete a longer and perhaps even sleeker version of the well-known shape. Entirely new door shells are required (the existing doors are much too long for their skins to be used as rear doors), though some existing hardware and detailing is often used, both to standardise and so that the conversion remains true to David Bache's original ideas.

In one way or another, several firms making special coachwork have had conversions approved by the company, including Herbert Lomas Ltd, Wadham Stringer (Coachbuilders) Ltd, and Pilcher-Greene Ltd, all of whom make ambulance conversions, while Gloster Saro Ltd make special fire crash tenders on Carmichael 6 × 4 long-wheelbase chassis for the Royal Air Force.

One of the better-known conversions (though it is not approved by the company, for legislative reasons) is built by A. E. Smith & Son Ltd, of Kettering, who are noted coachbuilders, and have supplied massive racing car transporters to firms like Elf Tyrrell and to Walter Wolf Racing. In this version, the standard front doors are retained, and the standard rear half of the shell including the original door shut face is also retained. Between there is a thicker than normal door pillar (called the B/C post in coachbuilders' language) on to which the new rear doors, relatively short compared with the original doors, are hung. When painted and decorated in the usual manner, it needs a second glance before the obvious and basic difference becomes apparent. In such cases, not only does the customer receive the undoubted advantage of having a four-door body, but he also gets a great deal of extra space in the rear seats. Since the front seat position is not changed, and since the rear seat folding mechanism stays in the same position relative to the rear wheel arch and the line of the back axle, it follows that all the wheelbase increase is added to the area ahead of the rear seats. In some specialised cases, 'occasional' folding seats, as often used in taxis or even in mayoral limousines, have been installed.

It is interesting to note that although wheelbase extensions are now popular on Range Rovers, they have never been in strong demand on Land-Rovers. However, in 1968 George Mackie's department was approached by the Greater London Council to develop a front-wheel-drive Land-Rover chassis for ambulance purposes (rear wheel components were to be discarded to allow a low loading platform to be provided). Work went on for some months, and included investigation into using Range Rover front axles, which have constant velocity joints, and into using the Range Rover power unit. Only after the project was terminated did ambulance body builders become aware of the new Range Rover project, and it was from there that the demand for wheelbase extensions, now carried out by Spencer Abbott (Engineers) Ltd, developed.

By comparison with such extension conversions, the work carried out on the two Range Rovers being prepared for an assault on the Darien Gap in Colombia, South America, seems minor, although a great deal of thought and previous expedition experience went into the job. Major John Blashford-Snell (and Captain Gavin Thompson, who led the actual vehicle party) took a 17th/21st Lancers expedition from Anchorage in Alaska to Ushuaia in Argentina—from the far north to the ultimate south of the American land mass—between December 1971 and June 1972. The actual crossing of the roadless and swamp-infested Darien Gap, between Panama City and Medellin in Colombia, took no fewer than 95 days, on the majority of which the Range Rovers needed to be man-handled, towed, pushed, or ferried, to gain any headway at all. That ninety-five days were spent covering no more than 250 miles gives an idea of the difficulty of the terrain.

Apart from thorough detailed preparation and checking of the standard mechanicals, the two expedition vehicles were given front winches, petrol tank undershields, exhaust system 'snorkels', split charge battery systems, swamp tyres, special dampers, roll cages, single reclining rear seats, cooker power points, built-in safes, water kegs, coffee makers, stowage lockers, full-length roof-racks, cow-catcher guards, extra lamps, instruments, roof mounted spare wheels, two-way radio installations, hand winches and ground anchors, extra towing eyes, sirens and air horns and many other detail fittings. Nevertheless, the engines were not especially modified for river crossings, and on at least one occasion a Range Rover was almost submerged after a near-capsize, and needed all its oils flushing out repeatedly before it could be used again.

Both these vehicles, which incidentally found the going really impossible at one point and needed replacement transmission parts air-dropped by RAF support craft, are now in the British Leyland Historic Vehicles Collection, based at Donington Park in Derbyshire.

The most special Range Rover of all, however, not for its equipment nor for its body style, but for its illustrious owner, is the unique convertible Range Rover manufactuded by the company at Solihull for delivery to the Queen in her Jubilee Year, 1977. Like the convertible Land-Rover, which made its debut in 1959, this Range Rover is arranged for the Sovereign to sit or stand in the rear compartment, so that she may use it as a mobile inspection vehicle, or may make parades in gatherings where a conventional Rolls-Royce from her fleet would not be appropriate.

Unlike the Range Rovers already described, this Royal vehicle is based on the standard chassis, with its 100in wheelbase, and with only two side doors. Its most important feature is that the roof and tail of the standard body, along with the side windows and the upper parts of the doors, have all been discarded. Frameless side windows are installed in the doors, and chauffeur and detective (or, in some cases, a senior police officer) sit on a sumptuously-trimmed bench seat which does not adjust, and which is backed by what amounts to a division.

The rear compartment has been completely gutted, and re-equipped. At each side there are metal blanking panels, topped by plain glass, and the division separating front and rear compartments is topped by a padded roll which Her Majesty can use for a hand-hold when travelling over unmade ground. Access to the rear compartment is from the rear of this very special Range Rover, by folding steps, and in it there are four inward-facing folding seats. As one would expect of a Royal vehicle, it is not registered, and is painted in a gorgeous and discreetly deep 'Imperial crimson'.

As with the Land-Rover, so with the Range Rover; there is probably

The Rover factory at Solihull in the late 1960s, before a start was made on the latest SD1 block. In the centre is the original 'shadow factory' building, much modified since the 1940s, and in which the whole of the Land-Rover and Range Rover final assembly took place until the early 1980s. To the left is what is colloquially known as the North Block, where Rover 2000 car production took place from 1963 to 1975. As part of Land-Rover Limited's bold expansion plans, announced in 1978, this building was converted to take over Range Rover assembly, and four-cylinder engine production. The gap between separate 'shadow factory' blocks was later closed, so that assembly lines could run straight through from one end to the other.

The SD1 block was completed on ground in the centre background of this shot, but Rover private car assembly ceased there in 1981, and in 1985 its conversion for Land-Rover/Range Rover component assembly was completed

no limit to the number of special jobs which a modified machine could be asked to perform. The one basic difference is that a Range Rover is a much more expensive purchase from which to begin modifications, and experience shows that this is the main reason why many local and national authorities have not yet applied the Range Rover chassis to their special tasks.

Motorway police patrol vehicles, AA/RAC recovery vehicles, ambulances, motor caravans, executive towing devices, cut-and-shut off-road racing projectiles, fire tenders, airport control vehicles, luxury estate or business transport, or merely expensive playthings have already been built on this splendid, fast, and luxurious base. No wonder Land-

Rover Limited are finding that demand continues to exceed supply, no matter how much the price has to be pushed up, and no matter how much a prospective customer may be discouraged by the nine-month waiting lists.

In recent years the potential competition to the Range Rover has become obvious. Monteverdi's look-alike competitor, the Safari, can only be built in minute quantities, and with its Chrysler/International chassis engineering was an expensive proposition. The new *Gelande-wagen* (land-vehicle) from Mercedes-Benz, launched in 1979, was commercially more significant. Even so, this vehicle did not take away many Range Rover customers in its first few years, possibly because of its looks, possibly because it lacked alloy panelling.

The Range Rover, however, was good enough, and successful enough, to stand up to anything being developed anywhere in the world. Expansion plans put in hand at Solihull not only included the long-expected launch of a diesel-engined version, but the ambitious assault on the vast North American market.

The final chapter details how this was done.

10 Building on Success

Although no new models were launched at Solihull in 1978, it was still a momentous year for what the traditionalists will always know as the Rover company. As a result of the financial and functional reorganisation approved by British Leyland's new chairman, Michael Edwardes, a separate company, Land-Rover Limited, was set up to capitalise on the phenomenal popularity of the Land-Rover and Range Rover families. Even more important was the news that the huge expansion rumoured so often in previous years was going ahead. By the early 1980s the Solihull scene will have changed considerably.

This book will already have made it clear that Rover could always sell every Land-Rover they could build, and that they could never build enough of them. In previous periods, management was cautious and thought that a healthy waiting list was acceptable; current thinking is that the highly profitable 4 × 4 models should be built and sold in much greater quantities.

When one surveys the great upheaval and the enormous amount of investment which is now going into the expansion programme, it is ironic to recall why the Land-Rover came into existence in the first place—it was meant to be a stopgap to help fill out the empty halls of the original 'shadow factory'! But ever since deliveries began in the summer and autumn of 1948 the company has been battling to keep up with the demand.

To explain the thinking behind the current expansion programme, I must backtrack to the Land-Rover's early years. In the late 1940s and early 1950s, Land-Rovers were built on assembly tracks alongside those where the luxurious P3 and P4 private cars were made. Many major components were delivered from other factories (engines and transmissions, for instance, came from the Acocks Green plant, just a couple of miles away, which was Rover's other wartime 'shadow factory', or from the Tyseley factory, which the company had owned since the end of World War I), or came from outside suppliers.

To deal with the insatiable demand for Land-Rovers *and* Rover private cars, and to push ahead with more and more production facilities for the future, every nook and cranny of the Solihull site was pressed into service. One result of this was that for many years the vital 'service' departments such as the design and development divisions, the top secret gas-turbine shops, tool rooms, and the various office buildings were all cramped for space themselves. It was not an ideal way for the company to face its future.

As far as the Land-Rover was concerned, the company's policy was that it should be kept as simple as possible, built on rudimentary assembly tooling, and, as far as possible, that everything should be manufactured 'in house'. For the private cars there was an entirely different policy, for Rover were quite happy to buy major components like chassis frames and complete body shells from specialist suppliers.

Without knocking down factory walls, however, there were practical limits to the numbers of Land-Rovers which could be built at Solihull. Without introducing a great deal of confusion and personal unhappiness it is not feasible continually to consider speeding up the pace of the assembly tracks, nor was it possible to extend the working week. Even by the beginning of the 1950s, when weekly production was up to 400 Land-Rovers a week, the buildings were bursting at the seams.

At this point industrial and financial logic clashed head on with government policy. During World War II Rover had very prudently bought up a lot of land around the Solihull site, and thought it obvious and logical that they should begin to expand the buildings outside their original confines. This would give space for more Land-Rovers to be built, for more exports to boost Britain's balance of payments, and for more men to be employed. The government, however, disagreed. Their policy was that industrial expansion should take place in development regions with existing (and historically persistent) high unemployment. Further, to enforce this policy they refused to issue development certificates (without which work could not go ahead on new construction) in prosperous areas like the West Midlands.

Rover were desperate, and in the face of this obduracy they had to change their plans. If Solihull could not be expanded, then certain previously 'in-house' processes would have to be moved out. If space could be released at Solihull, then more Land-Rovers could be assembled on duplicate lines. The problem was that the company would have to buy other premises in the area to take the overspill.

It was not an ideal solution, but it is one which has continued to this day. By the mid-1970s there were no fewer than eight Rover factories in the Birmingham area, and a large plant at Cardiff, along with a small operation in a side street in Coventry. This piecemeal expansion began in 1952 with the purchase of the Perry Barr factory, on the northern outskirts of Birmingham, which took over manufacture of Land-Rover front and rear axles. Two years later the Percy Road (Birmingham) building, a real Victorian period piece, was acquired, for the manufacture and assembly of Land-Rover gearboxes.

This was enough to look after Land-Rover expansion throughout the 1950s, and production steadily increased from 400 a week to around 800 a week. More than 30,000 Land-Rovers (actually 34,168) were built for the first time in 1959–60. At this point, however, the company was faced with further major expansion, and some critical policy decisions, to cope with the planned introduction of the entirely new generation of P6 (Rover 2000) private cars. There was no way that these cars could be assembled in the existing Solihull buildings, even though P4 production was to be phased out following the launch of P6.

Fortunately for the company, government policy had changed somewhat (as Rover's great rivals, Standard-Triumph, had also discovered at the end of the 1950s). Although the company wanted a major new building, and would have liked to site all of it at Solihull, they nevertheless accepted a compromise. A new final assembly building (the North Block) would be erected at Solihull, while they would also take over a large new factory at Pengam, near Cardiff, where P6 gearboxes and back axles would be made. Not, mind you, that this was the original, or even the intermediate plan. At one time it was proposed that Land-Rover assembly should be moved down to Cardiff, thus clearing Solihull again for private car assembly . . .

Demand for the Land-Rover, however, continued to increase, so with further Land-Rover expansion in mind more factories in the Birmingham area were taken over. In 1965 Tyburn Road and Garrison Street (both in Birmingham) were added to the line-up of valuable real estate. Garrison Street is another Victorian building, tucked away beside the railway embankment to the east of Birmingham's New Street station, and was used for many years to manufacture wire ropes for factories and collieries: now it is the centre of chassis frame production for the Land-Rover ranges, and houses that splendidly simple means of welding up 88in side members.

The first 1,000-a-week Land-Rover milestone was reached towards the end of the 1960s, by which time planning for Range Rover manufacture was well advanced. In 1969, and followed by a considerable reshuffle, the Tyseley No 2 factory (sited, as one might expect from its name, next door to the original Tyseley buildings) was added. There, for some years, the situation stabilised, even though Land-Rover production was pushed steadily up to the theoretical 1,400 per week mark, and even though the single Range Rover line could now produce up to 250 machines every week.

In the meantime, of course, the British Leyland combine had come into existence, and at first it was hoped that this would lead to higher profitability, more investment, and an early start on major expansion for the Land-Rover lines. But it was not to be. The company was squeezed between the world-wide oil crisis of 1973–4, and rising costs due to Britain's own domestic inflation (which had been accelerating since the end of the 1960s), and at the end of 1974 abruptly had to go cap in hand to the British government for financial aid.

The result was that aid was given, a Government committee (led by Lord Ryder) was asked to investigate British Leyland's affairs and future prospects, and within months the corporation had effectively become nationalised. The upheaval which followed included the dismissal of John Barber, the corporation's managing director, the retirement to Honorary President of Lord Stokes, and led to a wholesale turnover of executive staff at the Rover company. In the meantime, too, Rover had been drawing closer to Triumph since plans to merge the companies had been announced in 1972, and it is only fair to say that a mixture of confusion, disorientation, hope and despair was in evidence at Solihull for a while.

The Ryder Report had promised a great future for the nationalised company, which would be helped along by great chunks of public money, but at Solihull the only evidence of this, at first, was that the vast new assembly building for the new Rover SD1 private cars (the 2300/2600/3500 range) was speedily completed. The very successful P6 private cars (2200 and 3500 models) were dropped at Christmas 1975, and by the middle of 1976 the North Block, which had built these cars exclusively since 1963, had fallen silent and was empty.

From time to time in 1976 and 1977, Leyland's management let it be known that they were making plans to expand 4 × 4 production, and that the use of the North Block would enter into these plans. But no action followed to back up these fine words, principally because the corporation was still fighting to regain profitability, in a situation where investment capital was being eked out in the most critical areas. The Austin-Morris division of Leyland Cars, for instance, desperately needed new models—particularly a new small car—and for a time effort went into providing a new factory and new tooling for this 'Mighty Mini', along with the resources needed to get a new overhead camshaft engine on sale in all the medium-sized cars.

Finally, in the autumn of 1977, Leyland's Chairman, Sir Richard Dobson, was forced out of office. The government searched round for a new chairman—Leyland's fourth in three years—and took an embarrassingly long time to find one. Michael Edwardes agreed to a three-year secondment from Chloride Group Ltd, on his own terms, so that he could reorganise the concern in the way he thought best, without any political interference from the British government.

This, after a great deal of huffing and puffing, was granted, and the dynamic Edwardes set out undoing most of what the Ryder Report (which, in fairness, was based on many of the old private concern's plans) had recommended. In particular, he decided that the integrated monolith of Leyland Cars should once again be split into operating groups (something which had always been advised by executives of each group, but to no avail, in earlier years); from the summer of 1978 two autonomous companies came into being—Austin Morris Ltd, and Jaguar-Rover-Triumph Ltd. The latter group was also split into three companies—Jaguar Cars, Rover–Triumph Cars, and Land-Rover Limited. At last, and not before time, the 4 × 4 models were to be allowed to stand up and fight for themselves. Their profit performance could easily be measured, without being submerged in a mass of corporate figures.

Mike Hodgkinson, Land-Rover Limited's managing director, summed up the reason for this split very logically and succinctly:

It was felt that over the last 10—perhaps even 20—years the pressures on the main car divisions have meant that the potential of the Land-Rover has not properly been exploited. It was also felt that Land-Rover Limited should be set up as an entirely separate entity so that our customers (particularly those overseas, and don't forget that we export up to 80 per cent of our production) could see us standing on our own feet. In fact we now run the entire Solihull site, and the Rover–Triumph company is now a tenant of those areas in which it operates. We make our own engines, gearboxes and axles, and we also manufacture the V8 engines for distribution to the car companies which use it! We're also responsible for our own engineering, production engineering, quality control and product planning, along with sales and marketing.

At first it may seem strange that Land-Rover Limited should be aligned with the private car side of things, when in some ways the products have a lot in common with commercial vehicles built by Leyland Vehicles, but as there is much tradition, history and operating convenience connected with these links they are not likely to be altered. In any case Land-Rover/Range Rover components are either unique to these machines, or are shared with the private cars; there are no components shared with the trucks built elsewhere in the British Leyland empire.

Expansion plans made public in August 1978 mentioned a total investment to come of £280 million (at 1978 prices), of which the first £30 million had already been approved. Well before this book first appeared, this 'Stage 1' of the plan, which included launching the V8-powered Land-Rover, had enabled theoretical capacity of Land-Rover production to go up from 1,350 to 1,500 cars a week (in other words for perhaps nearly 7,000 more Land-Rovers to be built in a trouble-free year), and for Range Rover production to be boosted from a maximum of 300 a week to no less than 450 vehicles a week.

The Range Rover increase, in terms of the enormous prestige and the high price commanded by this excellent vehicle, was obviously of great importance. *The Daily Telegraph*, when reviewing these plans, summarised the situation perfectly:

> Leyland's failure to produce enough four-wheel drive vehicles has led to allegations of a black market in both Range Rovers and Land-Rovers, with buyers paying over the odds for early delivery.

Although Solihull's assembly lines had looked overcrowded for some years, the principal constraint on building more 4 × 4s had always been the limit to the number of engines and transmissions which could be manufactured. Stage I of the plan therefore involved a reshuffle in transmission-building resources, and concentrated on an expansion of V8 production capacity at Acocks Green.

Rover's V8 engine, of course, is one of the most versatile and successful in the British motor industry. Even though Rover took over the licence in 1965, and started manufacture in 1967, its potential has not been fully realised, though it has found a home in a whole variety of cars, and 4 x 4s. It is vital to Land-Rover Limited's strategy for many years to come, even though it will not be used in Rover private cars for much longer. Perhaps its most exciting use was in the Triumph TR7/TR8 family of sports cars. The expansion at Acocks Green, therefore, is only a start, and will allow 2,000 engines a week to be distributed throughout the corporation.

The magnificent light-alloy vee-8 engine, which did so much to liven up Land-Rover and Range Rover performance in the 1970s and 1980s, is here seen mated to the Range Rover's gearbox and transfer box

Allied to this, and coming on stream at the same time, was a replanning of facilities for the production of Range Rover gearboxes and central transmissions. Not only were more of these wanted so that more Range Rovers could be built, but the engine and the allied gearbox were also intended for fitment to the new line up of V8-powered Land-Rovers.

For the next few years, the bulldozers and the pneumatic drills were very active at Solihull. Whole departments – office staff, service blocks, and engineering workshops among them – were moved off site for a time to other rented buildings in the Solihull area, and for the very first time brand new assembly lines were laid down in the old 'shadow factory' buildings. By comparison with the 'traditional' cramped, Land-Rover facilities, the first new line was spacious and modern. For the first time, there was a covered way between two originally separated blocks, so that the first of the new models, the V8 Land-Rover, could start life as a bare frame at the western end of the complex, keep moving consistently in the same direction, and eventually roll out as a completed vehicle at the east end of the site.

In the meantime, as a time consuming temporary expedient, but to make the re-jigging possible, Land-Rover and Range Rover bodies were carted across the large factory site, a couple of hundred yards, by transporter, to the now redundant P6 paint shop in the North Block, painted, and then returned to the old 'shadow factory' for completion.

The net result, just at a time when the market peaked out, was that Solihull's final assembly capacity went up from a maximum of 1,650 4 x 4s a week, to 1,965 a week, while the major boost in engine building facilities at Acocks Green allowed 2,000, instead of 850, vee-8 engines to be manufactured every week.

Stage II, which followed, and came on stream in mid 1981, was a much more ambitious project. Not only did it give the old 'shadow factory' room to breathe for the first time in years, but it also brought Rover 4 x 4 assembly completely into modern times. It involved the complete takeover of the then empty P6 Rover assembly facility in North Block, and re-equipment for 4 x 4 production.

'Stage 1' of Land-Rover's re-equipment programme was the V8 Land-Rover model, still in the old type of leaf-spring chassis frame

First of all, the irregularities of the original building profile were filled out to make a good, basic, rectangular, factory and then the interior was gutted, the floors dug out as appropriate, and £85 million was spent on re-equipping it. That, incidentally, was probably more than had been spent on the entire Land-Rover project in the previous thirty years.

Half of the huge building was made into an ultra-modern engine machining, assembly, and testing plant for the Land-Rover's four-cylinder engines – petrol and diesel – while the other half was given over to complete Range Rover assembly. This meant that engine assembly progressively moved into Solihull from the old off-site facility, while the move for the Range Rover meant that more modernisation could be carried out (in advance of the One-Ten and Ninety launches) in the old 'shadow factory'.

The Range Rover assembly facility was now to be as modern as the product itself, and not before time, while the engine manufacturing plant was quite startlingly advanced – that is, by previous Land-Rover standards. Not only did it allow the new five-bearing crankshaft engine to be phased in (from 1981/2), but it also enabled an increase in engine size (from 2,286 to 2,495cc) on the diesel derivative.

Any industry observer looking at either facility would have been left in no doubt that Land-Rover Limited were planning for a long range future, and that the four-cylinder engine range as we know it still had

Really, the Range Rover body shell slots together in a very simple manner, as these jigs confirm. Later on, of course, it fills up completely with machinery!

many years to run. And that, according to all the Land-Rover enthusiasts I know, is a very good sign indeed. It would have been nice to see more powerful Land-Rovers (but that, surely, is what vee-8 engines are for?), but it was encouraging to know that continuity was assured too.

For the time being, at least, the satellite factories were retained (which must have been a relief to the workforce), even though many economic pundits (particularly some newspaper journalists) stated that they should be closed. At the time, though, Mike Hodgkinson explained:

> Sheer logic says that satellite factories make no sense, but they tend to be very efficient, have an existing very skilled workforce, good management, few labour relations problems, and a great deal of *esprit de corps* which somehow you just don't get in larger plants.
>
> Anyway, even if we ever *did* think of closing one down, we'd always find that the production could never be fitted in anywhere else.

Hodgkinson went on to stress that processes continued, and would continue, to be re-allocated from plant to plant, depending on the industrial logic of the moment. But it is a complex three-dimensional jig-saw, not conducive to revision by a desk-bound manager. As the managing director admitted:

> I couldn't possibly have undertsood all this without going on a complete tour as soon as I got this job. I'd been around the Solihull scene since 1971, but even so another long look was essential.

The problem of where to put facilities at Solihull if satellite factories were closed down, was not finally solved until 1983/84 (but that development really belongs to the next chapter).

Until the first of the coil-sprung Land-Rovers, the One-Ten, came on the scene in 1983, most of the headlines from Solihull were made by the launch of new Range Rover derivatives. In earlier chapters of this book, I recount how I have picked up 'wouldn't it be interesting if . . . ' ideas from Range Rover customers. Now, in the space of three or four years, most of the desirable changes were to be made.

The big demand had always been for a four-door derivative of the design, though this could only be satisfied, at great cost, by conversions; in the UK by companies like FLM Panelcraft, and Chris Humberstone Design, and in Switzerland by Monteverdi (the company which had, for a few years, built Chrysler-engined Supercars in the Jensen, and Iso mould). For a time, indeed, the Monteverdi conversion was approved, and marketed, by Land-Rover Limited, on the continent, and in the lucrative Middle East market.

The first factory-built four-door Range Rover came in 1981, eleven years after the vehicle had been launched. It immediately came to dominate the UK market sector, where boarding convenience was more important than cost

At the same time as the completion of the new North Block facilities were publicised, the company also chose to launch its own four-door version of the Range Rover, still on the same 100in wheelbase, and still with the same basic styling. Yet there were important mechanical and specification changes.

Right away, the four-door (which cost £750 more than the two-door, which was – and is – still available) took up the majority of sales in the UK, and soon came to dominate the assembly lines at Solihull. The new doors had recessed, Morris Marina style, door handles, while the rear seat was moved bodily backwards by three inches, which increased rear seat leg room, but cut back on stowage capacity in the rear.

At the same time there was an engine rethink. Originally, the Range Rover had been intended to use two star fuel, but now that there was virtually no price advantage in this, the big vee-8 engine was retuned for four star fuel (Super, on the continent). The compression ratio was raised to 9.35:1 (the same, in fact, as Rover private cars, which meant that the head machining and pistons could both be commonised), the camshaft timing was changed, the result being that peak torque was unchanged, and that there was a tiny loss of 5bhp, though the 125bhp was now developed at 4,000rpm instead of 5,000rpm. In other words, the engine was more flexible than ever before.

The opportunity was also taken to introduce changes to ensure a quieter gearbox, and the step-down ratios were modified to give higher overall gearing in high range. In addition, to counter criticism that the Range Rover, in general, had moved too far up market, a 'Fleetline' version was introduced, without power-assisted steering and some other fittings, and with a rubber floor covering, and PVC-trimmed seats. But, just to remind the world of the luxuries which could be built into a Range Rover, the first 'In Vogue' version, a 1,000-off limited edition developed in conjunction with the coach builders, Wood & Pickett, was also put on sale.

There was more to come. From the summer of 1982, the first Range Rovers with automatic transmission were introduced, and a year later the machine was given a five-speed transmission. The automatic was a Chrysler (USA) design, the Torqueflite found in cars like the Aston Martin V8, and in most Chrysler USA products while the five speeder

The option of automatic transmission, from 1982, was a real advance for the Range Rover, whose plush image deserved such touches. This particular car also has in-dash air-conditioning – essential in hot climates such as the Middle East

The four-door Range Rover lost nothing in its re-styling, for it was still a handsome multi-purpose model, with peerless cross-country performance. This example also shows off the 1984 facelift, including the one-piece front side windows

was a much-modified version of the gearbox used in the current Rover hatchbacks, and in the Series III Jaguar XJ6 saloons. In both cases, the high and low ranges of gearing were retained.

The automatic was as smooth, and unobtrusive, as one might expect – when I tried one in truly awful cross-country conditions, I found that this type of Range Rover still had the same, near-unstoppable abilities. The five speeder brought two improvements to Range Rover motoring: one, the geared-up fifth gear offered truly high-geared, re-laxed, cruising (for it was rated at 25.8mph/1,000rpm, instead of the 20.0mph/1,000rpm of the original machine, a near thirty per cent cut in engine revolutions), and two, the actual gear-change quality was much improved.

Even though the world demand for 4 x 4s (particularly the expensive variety) slumped badly in the early 1980s, this series of changes helped the Range Rover considerably. In 1980 9,708 Range Rovers had been built, but in 1982 this rose sharply to 13,255, and even in recession-hit 1983 the figure was 12,182. It was also clear that Range Rover custo-

From mid-1984 the Range Rover received a new facia layout, including seg-
mented instruments, a more 'car-like' centre console, and completely relocated
dials and switchgear. Note the cloth-covered seats, the in-dash air-conditioning,
and the radio loudspeaker grilles in the door trim panels

mers still wanted the best, the most luxurious, and the most completely
equipped model, if they could afford it. A tour of the final assembly
lines in 1984 was notable for showing the high proportion of vehicles
with in-dash air-conditioning, the In Vogue trim pack (which became a
regular option, once the special limited edition had sold out), alloy road
wheels – and, of course, the four-door shell; by this time, more than
ninety per cent of all UK sales were of the four-door variety.

All this improvement in sales, incidentally, had been achieved without a major visual facelift, and this finally came along in mid-1984.
Still quite unmistakeable in its general proportions, and still on the same
sturdy 100in wheebase, the Range Rover now received a completely
revised facia and instrument layout, reclining front seats, improved ventilation, one-piece side windows, electronic engine ignition, power-
assisted steering as standard on all models, and many other equipment
changes and improvements. The Range Rover for the mid-1980s, therefore, was better, and more attractive, than ever before. Statistics showed
that it was selling faster than ever in the UK (where the ludicrous waiting

lists had finally disappeared), though worldwide sales were still badly
hit by the recession in some important export territories, particularly the
Middle East, where oil revenues had declined sharply since the beginning of the decade.

It was a blessing for Land-Rover Limited management that this sort
of vehicle does not need re-styling every five years or so to help stimulate
demand. Quality of construction, go-anywhere ability, and long-life
prospects, are much more important, and the Range Rover has those
in great abundance. It was a source of real pleasure to management
when, in 1984, Britain's most waspish motoring magazine, *Car*, carried
out a joint exercise with the USA's *Car & Driver*, on all available big-
engined 4 x 4s, and came to the conclusion that: 'Out of it all emerged
the superiority of the Range Rover'.

Managing Director Mike Hodgkinson moved on to another industrial
post at the end of 1982, and was replaced by Tony Gilroy, a manufacturing engineering specialist, who had already made his name by taking
the Austin Metro from an idea to a 4,000 a week production reality at
Longbridge, then moving into the Freight Rover premises in Birmingham, to sort out, revitalise, and effectively relaunch the Sherpa light
commercial vehicle.

Gilroy, encouraged by the chairman of Leyland Vehicles, David
Andrews, was brimming over with confidence, and the events of 1983
and 1984 must have been satisfying for him. On the assumption that
the Range Rover, in its present styling form, would be around for some
years to come, there were two major imponderables to be considered
– the persistent rumours that the vehicle should go on sale in the USA,
and the long-running (and still unrequited) need for a diesel-engined
vee-8 alternative.

Studies into the USA possibilities for Range Rover were still 'on
going', as the Americans themselves would say, the two stumbling
blocks being the cost of modifying the design to meet all the legislative
requirements in that market, and the complete lack of a suitable distribution network. If the Rover 3500, launched into the USA with such
confidence in 1980, had succeeded, and if the vee-8 powered Triumph
TR8 sports car was also still on the market, distribution would not be
a problem. As it is, the Rover 3500 flopped badly, and the TR8 was
withdrawn at the end of 1981.

The lack of a suitable diesel engine was sad, and must have been
hurting the Range Rover's sales. In the early 1980s the company had

mounted an expensive programme, in conjunction with Perkins, called the 'Iceberg' project, which was to convert the existing vee–8 engine to diesel specification, but that programme persistently failed to come up to scratch, and the entire project was cancelled in 1984. Yet all the Range Rover's main competitors had diesel-engined options, and there was no way that Solihull could continue to ignore this market sector. Nothing daunted, therefore, Tony Gilroy's team started again, but the new derivative would not be put on sale until 1986.

In the meantime, sales continued to increase at a satisfying, if not sensational, rate. The 150,000th Range Rover was produced during 1986, and demand continued to increase. Where would it all end? In the case of the Land-Rover, of course, it never did.

11 Ninety and One-Ten —
the Modern Generation

At the core of the ambitious Land-Rover Limited expansion scheme was the development, and launch, of an entirely new family of Land-Rovers. Everyone, and especially the designers at Solihull, knew that the original Jeep-based concept had been out-dated by the passage of time.

Even Tom Barton, whose philosophy regarding hard suspension, and a limit to cross-country speeds, to preserve the chassis frame itself, was well-known, knew what had to be done. Refer to pages 88 to 90, based on an interview taken in the mid-1970s, for evidence that almost everything had been thought of by that time. From time to time prototypes had been built, tested, modified, then put on one side. Until the investment capital was made available, nothing further could be done.

Now the time was ripe. Management and designers knew what they wanted to achieve, and effectively how that should be done. Technically, a new Land-Rover needed more wheel movement, and more supple suspension, though the existing engine line-up, suitably improved, was still right for the job.

It would have been nice to extend the range down and up the payload range, but the downward move was not cost-effective. Thus it was possible to offer Land-Rovers with a bigger payload and more capacity for big loads, and this was taken into account.

The styling, too, needed freshening up. At one time a completely new body shell (still in aluminium panels) was considered, but eventually it was decided to retain the familiar shape (with a huge choice of styles), to freshen up the front end, and to allow for wider wheel tracks to be standard. In addition, it was decided to provide a much more car-like facia and instrument layout.

Well-proven prototypes existed by 1978 when I had my first confidential look at the 1979-model V8 Land-Rover, though the factory conversion work, and all the tooling for the new models, would not be ready until 1983. In the meantime, two important scene-setting interim models were produced on the basis of the existing leaf-spring Series III chassis. One was the High Capacity pick-up truck, while the other was the more completely trimmed County station wagon.

The High Capacity model, on the 109in wheelbase, could carry a payload of 1.3 tonnes, while the County station wagons – 88in or 109in wheelbase derivatives – had special paint jobs, and more equipment, and specification details. The short-wheelbase versions had seven seats, the 109in wheelbase examples twelve seats.

Then, in March 1983, the new One-Ten was launched. It made its debut at the Geneva motor show of that month (initial sales, in any case, were concentrated on the export market), but it was a great pity that, as far as the newspapers in this country were concerned, its arrival was quite overshadowed by the launch of the new Austin Maestro. Make no mistake about this: the One-Ten was, as the factory publicists insisted, the most significant development of the Land-Rover since its launch 35 years earlier.

The design of the new One-Ten (the model name, incidentally, indicated that its wheelbase was 110in, just one inch more than that of the longer-wheelbase Series III Land-Rover) included everything the pundits

A 'ghosted' view of the One-Ten station wagon of 1983, showing coil spring suspension all round, the front wheel disc brakes and, in this case, the vee-8 engine

had been demanding for so long. Central to the design was a sturdy, all-new, chassis frame, similar in concept to that of the Range Rover but quite different in detail, box-section and robot-welded, and no less

The big change for the One-Ten/Ninety series of Land-Rovers was that they were given coil spring suspension and front-wheel disc brakes. At a stroke, the new suspension turned the Land-Rover from a bone-crushing extrovert into a much more refined and versatile cross-country 4 x 4

than 7.5in deep in the centre section, where strength was most needed.

As before, there was permanent four-wheel drive, and beam front and rear axles, but for the One-Ten suspension was by vertical coil springs, with co-axial dampers; front suspension location was by radius arms and a Panhard rod, rear location by radius arms and an A-bracket. At the rear there was a Boge Hydromat self-levelling strut which was standard on County station wagons and optional on all other derivatives.

Not only that, but for the very first time on a Land-Rover, the specification included front wheel disc brakes, with vacuum servo assistance.

This specification, allied to much increased available wheel movements (7.0in at the front, 8.5in at the rear) meant that the suspension could be made much softer than that of the Series III, and this meant that the wheels could be in contact with the ground (and therefore, still pushing or pulling) more of the time, at higher speeds. The Series III had had remarkable traction but the One-Ten was just superlative!

In a go-anywhere contest between the SIII and the Range Rover, the Range Rover would usually win. Now, if the One-Ten was brought into such a battle, I suspect the result would be an honourable, and amazing, draw.

The line up of power units was exactly as expected, though there were power boosts all round – 74bhp from the $2\frac{1}{4}$-litre petrol 'four', 60bhp from the equivalent diesel, and no less than 114bhp from the vee-8. For the One-Ten, however, the four-cylinder cars were treated to the new LT77 five-speed gearbox (with a geared-up fifth) – basically the same as that used in the Rover and Jaguar executive saloons, though with different ratios – while the vee-8 engined cars retained the Range Rover type LT95 four-speed box.

Incidentally, though the LT77 was certainly man enough to look after the 190bhp of the vee-8 engine, when installed in the Rover Vitesse car, it could not adequately withstand the shock-loadings and torque-reversals imposed on it when linked to the less-powerful vee-8 in the One-Ten, so that engine had to use the old Range Rover transmission for the time being. As before, the Range Rover-based transmission was in permanent four-wheel-drive, whereas the four-cylinder cars could have rear-wheel, or four-wheel-drive, and in all cases there was a choice between high (normal) or low range gearing.

To top off this new chassis, the wheel tracks were considerably widened (at 4ft 10.5in), which meant that flexible wheel arch extensions,

Styling of Land-Rovers changes only slowly. The V8 model of 1979 had been given the flush-front nose style, which was carried forward for the One-Ten (seen here) and the Ninety models of the early 1980s. In addition, the One-Ten and Ninety models had wider wheel tracks, and flexible plastic wheel arch 'eyebrows'. To a Land-Rover customer of the 1950s, however, it is still all very familiar

in deformable plastic, were needed, while power-assisted steering was optional on all models.

Like the Land-Rover V8, the One-Ten had a flush-front form of styling, while the interior was much more 'car-like' than any previous Land-Rover. Not only was a Range Rover-like four-spoke steering wheel fitted, but there were altogether more civilised-looking facia and instruments. The speedometer, incidentally, read up to 120mph, in spite of there being no chance of attaining that velocity, even with the 114bhp vee-8 engine fitted!

The most important thing to be remembered was that none of the traditional Land-Rover go-anywhere/do-anything features had been abandoned, and, if anything, there was even more corrosion-proof aluminium panelling in the body shells than ever.

I revelled in a full day's test driving of all the new types when they were announced, wished that power-assisted steering could have been standard, but otherwise enthused on this better-than-ever specification.

What luxury for a Land-Rover! This is the One-Ten (and the Ninety is the same), complete with its new five speed all-synchromesh transmission, a clock, and a positively car-like instrument layout. The steering wheel style should be familiar to Range Rover owners

One-Ten, in fact, had only arrived in the nick of time as Land-Rover Limited's business was in the process of taking a real hammering. The bald facts show that annual production figures had been steadily declining during the 1980s, though in 1985, finally, the production rate turned up again. There were several reasons for this at Solihull.

One was certainly that the buying public was becoming bored with the old SIII, and therefore likely to look around at the competition (particularly the Japanese), but the upheavals in the world's economy caused by the huge increase in oil prices in 1978/79 also had an enormous effect.

Britain, plunged into recession, did not suffer too disastrous a sales drop, but Nigeria found that it could not finance overseas trade once the world stopped buying its expensive oil, while many Middle East contracts had to be spread out (and purchase of working vehicles deferred) to match income to expenditure. As one Land-Rover Limited spokesman told me: 'We used to sell up to around 3,000 a year in Nigeria, but in 1984 we sold just a handful.'

Not only did this decline, which Land-Rover executives insist was mostly unstoppable, hit hard at company profitability but it also made the expansion look ludicrously over-optimistic. Whereas Range Rover production has been knocking up hard against its single-shift capability of 300 cars a week for some time, the Land-Rover lines themselves have been working at little more than one-third of their capacity for two worrying years.

When the expansion plan work commenced, Land-Rover Limited forecast that the worldwide 4 x 4 market would continue to grow at five per cent every year, as it always seemed to have done – but within two years that forecast was completely knocked out of court. The company now admits, too, that they could sell more vehicles if they had a cheaper, smaller, and simpler model, but then they have never been in this sort of market, and it would take another huge investment project to make it possible.

All of which explains why the next step forward, to produce a short-wheelbase version of the One-Ten, was extremely important to the company, both in the short and the long term. The Land-Rover watchers, in any case, did not have to wait long, for the new vehicle, called Ninety, was introduced in June 1984, just 15 months after the arrival of the One-Ten.

Ninety was almost exactly what might have been expected, except for one rather important detail – the wheelbase was *not* 90 in. The first prototypes, apparently, had used that dimension, but the production Ninety actually had a wheelbase of 92.9in. Apart from the short chassis itself – which, as on other Land-Rovers, meant that the load platforms were shorter, for ahead of the rear bulkhead to the front seats, the two vehicles were the same – many of the One-Ten's newly-developed components were used.

During the winter of 1983/84, the four-cylinder diesel engine had been enlarged, to 2,495cc by using a longer stroke, and a peak power output of 67bhp; already line-fitted to the One-Tens, it was now one of the standard engines for the Ninety. The only other engine, at this time, was the 2,286cc petrol 'four'. This meant that every Ninety came equipped with the LT77 five speed transmission. Other features like the coil spring suspension, the optional power-assisted steering, and the front-wheel disc brakes, were all specified, and there was the usual large choice of body styles, and optional equipment.

Nice details, also standardised on One-Ten at the same time, included

The up-market County station wagons made their debut in 1982 on the Series III models, but there is now a County for the Ninety and One-Ten ranges as well. Cloth seats, full trim and instrumentation, special paint and decoration schemes, and larger-section or radial ply tyres were all part of the specification

wind-up windows in the front passenger doors, and on station wagons an electrically heated rear window, and a wash-wipe installation.

The Land-Rover, of course, had come a long way from the original 1948 model. So, of course, had price levels in general, but there was no doubt that the Ninety and One-Ten models were altogether more up-market, and better-equipped, than the originals. In 1984, the 7-seater petrol-engined Ninety station wagon cost £9,212 – compare that with the price of an 80in Land-Rover of 1948 – £450!

The final plank in the modernisation programme did not fit in until the spring of 1985, but I must first explain the background by mentioning Santana (more exactly Metalurgica de Santa Ana SA), of Spain, which is the only company outside Solihull which actually builds Land-Rovers from scratch.

Santana has been in existence since 1955, has been building Land-Rovers since 1959, and has been gradually evolving Land-Rover derivatives quite separate from the UK variety. Some of the design is local Spanish, some Solihull-based, but one thing is absolutely certain – the

Spanish product is a fine Land-Rover, and Solihull readily acknowledges this.

One major design job tackled by Santana in the 1970s was the production of straight six-cylinder derivatives (3,429cc) of the existing Solihull four-cylinder units, but an even more important 'building block', introduced in 1983, was a five-speed gearbox with all the torque capabilities of the rather truck-like four-speed box used in the Range Rover, and other vee-8 engined 4 x 4s assembled at Solihull.

So it was that in the spring of 1985, Santana and Solihull came together again, this time with the Ninety and One-Ten models in mind. Not only was a 114bhp vee-8 engine fitted to the Ninety (making that the very first short-wheelbase Land-Rover to be fitted with a vee-8 engine by the factory, though such transplants had been carried out by 4 x 4 enthusiasts many times previously), but that engine was also able to be backed by a five-speed gearbox – what the company called the LT85 unit, but what was actually the five-speed, all-synchromesh unit tooled and produced by Santana in Spain. Like the LT77 box, though entirely different from it, the new transmission had an overdrive fifth gear. ·

There was still an anomaly between Land-Rover and Range Rover models, which the development engineers could only explain in terms of shock loadings, all-up weights, and other 'we test everything and then

Squeezing the 3.5-litre vee-8 engine into the front of the Land Rover Ninety was not easy, but there was a place for everything, and this was the fastest Land-Rover so far offered, available from 1985

decide if it's good enough' attitudes. The four-cylinder Land-Rovers had the LT77 'car-type box', and the vee-8 Land-Rovers the LT85 from Spain. The vee-8 Range Rovers, however, had the LT77 box. Illogical? Maybe, but nothing is left to chance at Solihull.

The jigsaw was almost complete, and by the end of 1985 it would be quite ready for inspection. Late in 1983 came the news that the company had changed its mind about 'satellite' factories and that the redundant, mothballed, 'SDI' car-production building alongside the Land-Rover facilities at Solihull had been taken over from the Austin Rover Group with rationalisation in mind. By closing down nine off-site facilities, almost all of them old premises, and transferring their manufacturing capability to the SDI building, it was claimed that savings of £14 million a year would be made.

By the end of 1985, it was suggested, not only would the last military contracts for Series III Land-Rovers have been fulfilled at Solihull (which meant that every 4 x 4 being assembled at Solihull would have coil spring suspension, and modern assembly techniques), but the SDI building would be full, and humming with activity, producing mechanical components of myriad types. For the first time since 1948, 4 x 4 assembly, *in toto,* would be concentrated on the one massive industrial site at Solihull.

The Land-Rover, however, had now been around for a very long time indeed, so it was not at all surprising that by the mid-1980s most of Solihull's headlines were being developed by the more glamorous Range Rover. In spite of the fact that the coil-sprung Land-Rovers were more advanced, and more modern, than the faithful old Series III models had been, they were not selling as well as before. One reason – the economic collapse of some previous Land-Rover 'best-seller' markets – has already been mentioned, but another was that the competition, especially from Japanese products, was getting more fierce with every season which passed. Change, and improvement, had to be pushed ahead as rapidly as possible.

At this time, visitors to Solihull must surely have noticed that the four-cylinder petrol and diesel powered engines were all machined and assembled on the same facilities, so in 1984–1985 it made no obvious sense that the two engines were being built in different sizes. From the autumn of 1985, this anomaly was removed, with the petrol engine being enlarged from its long-established 2,286cc (this had been a Solihull 'standard' size for 27 years!), to 2,495cc. This meant that peak power rose from 74bhp to 83bhp, but more importantly it meant that peak torque (or 'lugging power') went up from 120lbft to 133lbft.

So far, so good, but it was also high time that the diesel engine should receive some attention. In 1961, when the 2,286cc diesel engine had been introduced, it produced 62bhp, and a quarter of a century later its 2,495cc development produced 73bhp. In the meantime, however, the weight of a typical long-wheelbase Land-Rover had soared from 3,300lb to 3,800lb – which meant that it was a less lively car even than the 1961 example.

It was time for a boost – literally – and from October 1986 one became available. For the short-wheelbase Ninety, and the longer-wheelbase One-Ten ranges, alike, a turbocharged version of the 2,495cc diesel engine was made optionally available, this being the very first 'in house' turbo produced by Solihull's engineers.

Not only did the new derivative use the same sort of Garrett AiResearch turbo as was found in high-performance car installations, but it had a revised crankshaft and a more rigid cylinder block. This all helped to boost peak power *and* peak torque by a quarter, to 85bhp and 150lbft respectively. Compared with the normally-aspirated diesel engine, this muscly new unit added only £446 – or a mere four per cent – to the selling price, which looked like a real bargain to many customers.

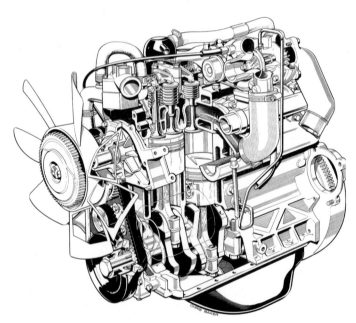

Not before time, the turbocharged version of the Land-Rover's four-cylinder engine was launched in 1986. The cylinder block, and the crankshaft, were stiffened up, to cope with the extra power

By the mid-1980s, the coil-sprung One-Ten models were beginning to attract military orders from all around the world. This machine is seen, under test, by the Australian army

Not even the extra performance of this engine, however, could overcome the sheer size and bulk of the latest Land-Rovers, for road tests showed that top speed was stuck at 74mph (those aerodynamics again!), whereas overall fuel consumption was around 20mpg, and this highlighted the on-going problem with the Land-Rover – that there was a very difficult balance to be struck between vehicle performance, on the one hand, and structural strength, and therefore weight, on the other.

It was to deal with this, as far as possible, that the optional vee–8 engine also received a boost for 1987. With peak power rising from 114bhp at 4,000rpm, to 134bhp at 5,000rpm, it was, and felt like, a much more responsive engine than before.

The fact was, however, that by 1987 the Land-Rover's image, and its sales, were in the doldrums. In 1986, only 22,026 vehicles were sold, this being the lowest figure the famous 4×4 had achieved for more than 30 years. Although military sales – always an important factor in Land-Rover sales over the years – were gradually being won again, it was a worrying time for the management team at Solihull.

It was no secret that Britain's government was keen to see the Land-

Rover Ltd business sold off, or 'privatised', for it was almost entirely self-contained, and did not depend on any other part of the BL (now Rover Group) group for its facilities. It was also clear that this was not likely to happen until the company was much more profitable than it had been in recent years. By the late-1980s, of course, other sections of the state-owned Rover Group combine – notably Jaguar, Unipart, and Leyland Vehicles – had already been sold off, and Land-Rover must surely follow.

Land-Rover enthusiasts, I feel sure, would be delighted to see 'their' company sold off, especially as control by British Leyland, and later by the state, had been stifling, in the extreme, for a number of years. Many people, indeed, were convinced that Land-Rover's product quality, and character, would be enhanced by such a change. They are, in any case, looking ahead to the future, to see what sort of surprises the company has in store for us all. The company has surprised us all before. It can do so again.

The new-generation forward-control Land-Rover, revealed in 1986 in prototype form. Much smoother styling than previous types

12 Range Rover – expansion, and assault on the USA, in the mid–1980s

When the Land-Rover was first introduced, in 1948, most four-wheel-drive machines were bought as workhorses, but by 1970, when the Range Rover came along, all that had changed. A new type of customer, the sporting and leisure user, was apparent. It was soon obvious that many 4×4s were rarely used in 'off-road' conditions; the most difficult job tackled by most of them was to pull a horsebox out of a slippery grass field at a point-to-point meeting.

By the mid-1980s, the demand for up-market 4×4s had expanded considerably, and the Range Rover was ideally placed to satisfy this. Ten years earlier, the company had been quite happy to sell 300 Range Rovers every week – the capacity limit of the original assembly lines – which was well below potential sales, and they did not have to worry too much about developing more derivatives to satisfy every need. It was now necessary to fill out the range, and to make the choice as wide as possible.

As I have already recounted in an earlier chapter, between 1981 and 1984 a lot of work had already been done. The first four-door Range Rover had been announced in 1981, an automatic transmission option had appeared in 1982, and a five-speed transmission had taken over from the original four-speeder in 1983. Then, in mid-1984, an important face-lift had been unveiled, featuring a new facia style, and one-piece side-windows.

There was still, however, a great deal which *could* be done, and at this time the three important projects which were buzzing around Solihull can be summarised briefly as – more performance, a diesel engine option, and the North American market.

When the Range Rover reached its fifteenth birthday, in June 1985, it was still no faster than ever, and only marginally more economical than it had been in the early 1970s. The vee-8 engine's power unit was actually *less* powerful – 125bhp (DIN) in the early 1980s, compared with 135bhp (DIN) in the early 1970s – and it was a very lucky Range Rover owner who could achieve more than 15mpg (Imperial) from his car.

In 1985, as in 1970, the car's top speed was, and always had been, around 95mph, with 0–60mph acceleration in about 14 seconds. When the Range Rover had been new, this sort of performance had been thought outstanding, but rival cars were now beginning to catch up. In many ways the Range Rover's chassis was still under-exploited, for in spite of its weight, height, and general bulk the car had good road manners, excellent brakes, and good overall stability. Various conversions, including engines turbocharged by Janspeed, had shown that it could certainly cope with more power.

Ever since BL's chairman, Sir Michael Edwardes, had de-centralised the various businesses, to encourage them to develop separately, Land-Rover Ltd had effectively become the 'owners' of the vee-8 engine design. At this time the 'works' BL Cars competitions department developed a series of ultra-powerful, and very reliable, vee-8 engines, first for use in the rallying Triumph TR7 V8s, and later for use in Rover 3500 saloons which were used in racing and rallying.

To make the Rover an even better racing car, Austin-Rover then developed the Vitesse saloon, which was put on sale in October 1982. It was the Vitesse engine tune – 190bhp (DIN) at 5,280rpm, with the aid of Lucas 'L' electronic fuel injection – which was to prove so useful to Land-Rover in the next few years.

Even so, it was not until the autumn of 1985 that the first fuel-injected Range Rover, the 1986-model Vogue, was put on sale, a car which was also distinguished by further re-touching to the style, and by

The Range Rover finally got a more powerful fuel-injected engine option in 1985, with peak power of 165bhp. The basic installation was the same as that used in the Rover Vitesse car. USA-market Range Rovers had this engine, but 150bhp when running on un-leaded fuel

The 1986-model Vogue, seen fording a shallow water-splash, shows that the new front spoiler is much nearer ground (or water!) level than ever before

the offering of a different transmission. The company chose to launch this derivative in some style, by inviting scores of dealers and influential journalists to try the latest type in cross-country courses linking the stately homes of Althorp House, near Northampton, and Woburn Abbey, near Milton Keynes, with fast sections of dual carriageway road in between.

Under the bonnet of the latest Vogue was a fuel-injected engine which looked very similar indeed to that which had been used by the Rover Vitesse car in recent years, for it used the same type of inlet manifold/plenum chamber. Although it was by no means as powerful or as 'peaky' as the Vitesse's engine – 165bhp instead of 190bhp, with maximum power developed at lower revs – it was no less than 30 per cent more powerful than the carburetted-engine used in other Range Rovers.

This meant that, for the very first time, here was a Range Rover with a top speed of more than 100mph. Independent tests, in fact, showed that this new car could reach about 105mph and, perhaps even more importantly, that it could reach 60mph from rest in 11.9 seconds. The miracle of all this was that it was no less economical than before – *Autocar* testers recorded overall fuel consumption of 15.0mpg.

Even then, it was expected that this fuel-injected engine would soon account for the majority of all Range Rover sales, and this soon proved to be the case. From the end of 1986, in fact, the fuel-injected engine was standardised on *all* four-door Range Rovers, the old-type carburettor engine being continued on the small number of two-door models still being produced.

The other major mechanical innovation, introduced at the same time, was a new and up-to-date optional automatic transmission. The *original* Range Rover automatic transmission, introduced in 1982, was the Chrysler Torqueflite unit, built in North America, which had three forward ratios, with a direct 'top' gear. Although this, at the time, was a 'state-of-the-art' design, one which was eventually ordered by 40 per cent of Range Rover customers, and one which had been used on cars like the current Aston Martin and Lagonda models, it was neither as smooth in operation, nor as fuel efficient as new designs known to be on the way.

Accordingly, when the fuel-injected Vogue engine was introduced, it was time for a new type of automatic transmission to be offered. This was the latest West German ZF design – the 4HP22 unit – which was not only a four-speed unit, but one which had a 'lock-up' clutch for use with the 0.73:1 'overdrive' fourth gear, and the ability to lock-up in first gear for very steep off-road descents.

Range Rover, incidentally, were in very good company when they adopted this ZF automatic, for the same basic transmission was also available in the new-style Jaguar XJ6 and BMW 730i/735i luxury saloons.

To match the mechanical changes (which also included the re-tailoring of the suspension to reduce roll on hard cornering, and the use of a new direct gearchange linkage to the five-speed manual transmission), the Range Rover also inherited modified switchgear and control positions on the facia/instrument panel, and the addition of a deep moulded polyurethane front spoiler, to the nose of the car.

All this product action, however, involved further price increases. From October 1985, Range Rover prices in the UK started at £13,632 for the stripped-out 'Fleetline' model, and rose to no less than £18,696 for the fuel-injected Vogue. With automatic transmission available at £997, and other options also available, it was now quite normal for dealers to deliver new 1986-model Range Rovers with the 'bottom line' of the invoice exceeding £20,000. This, let me remind you, was ten times what it had originally been in 1970. . . .

Even so, by this time the Range Rover's reputation was so high, and its regular clientele so affluent, that price levels no longer seemed to be

From the autumn of 1985, the Range Rover was offered with a fuel-injected version of the vee-8 engine, and with optional *four*-speed ZF automatic transmission. Note, too, the new deep air dam incorporated in the front bumper, complete with low-mounted driving lamps – much more Kings Road than cross-country, I feel. . . .

a critical factor. Although a Fleetline Range Rover, with two passenger doors and rather less luxurious trim, remained in the lists, it sold very slowly – the vast majority of all Range Rovers being ordered were Vogues, often loaded up with options such as automatic transmission and air-conditioning.

It was the conclusions of the *Autocar*'s road test which summed up the situation so well:

'After over 15 years in production, the Range Rover is still a unique product. There are certainly cars that command more prestige . . . but there is still nothing that combines highway comfort and off-road ability so well . . . It might look much the same as it did in 1970, but the latest Range Rover Vogue is a much-improved beast . . . where else can you buy a car that's at home in both the directors' car park and the farmyard?'

The great joy of this latest Range Rover was that it was such an easy machine to drive – on *and* off the road. At the press launch of the fuel-injected Vogue, which featured a varied test route, up hill and down dale, across the deer park of Althorp, and through the woods around Woburn Abbey, I persuaded my wife to take the wheel. Although she had never even sat behind the wheel of a Range Rover before this occasion, she settled down to enjoy it almost at once, and that included whisking me along dual carriageway roads at speeds that I had not previously experienced in this massive four-wheel-drive machine. . . .

The next Range Rover development, however, was of a very different nature. Whereas the 1986-model Vogue was always intended to make the Range Rover a more glamorous machine, the launch of a diesel-engined version, in April 1986, was aimed at making it more versatile than ever.

Until petrol prices suddenly went 'through the roof' at the end of the 1970s, there was little need for Land-Rover designers to consider using a diesel engine in the Range Rover. Its customers, they reasoned, were perfectly happy to put up with the 12–15mpg thirst of the petrol engined types, as the price of having a silent, flexible, and torquey vee-8 engine.

By the early 1980s, however, the balance had shifted considerably. Not only were more and more people becoming interested in fuel-efficiency, but in many countries diesel fuel prices were much lower than those for petrol.

Land-Rover Ltd therefore set out on an ambitious programme, along with the British diesel-engine specialists, Perkins, to 'dieselise' the vee-8 engine. This was the 'Iceberg' project, which involved producing completely new cylinder heads, and stiffening up the cylinder block and crankshaft. For a time it looked as if this engine might be useful for the Range Rover, and for car makers who were also seeking a diesel engine option.

It was a good idea, but it did not work out. Initial results, apparently, were encouraging, but it soon became clear that a 'conversion' was not going to work satisfactorily. The main problem was that the vee-8 petrol engine had a light-alloy cylinder block, which was not only light in weight, but was also a very efficient transmitter of engine noises. So much work was needed on the previously-dedicated petrol-engine layout, or would have been needed on production tooling, that the whole project became uneconomic.

[Not only Land-Rover Ltd suffered this sort of setback. At the same time, Jaguar were also tempted to develop a diesel-engined version of their brand-new six-cylinder engine, for use in the next-generation XJ6 models – and this project, too, was cancelled. . . .]

The only sensible course was to cancel the project, and start again. A great deal of time had already been lost, but since this occurred at a time when Range Rovers were still selling as fast as they could be assembled at Solihull, perhaps the commercial damage was limited.

Managing director Tony Gilroy decided not to start another 'in-house' project, but instructed his engineers to scour the world's motor industry for a suitable design which could be 'bought-in', perhaps after a joint development programme had been concluded. It would be the very first time that a Land-Rover, or a Range Rover, was to be powered by an 'outside-supply' engine.

Even when the fuel-injected Vogue was launched, in the autumn of 1985, when he was questioned about a diesel-engined programme, Tony Gilroy insisted that evaluation was still proceeding, but we now know that this was a diplomatic way of saying 'mind your own business – we will tell you when we are ready. . . .' It was a white lie. In fact the diesel-engined Range Rover was announced in April 1986, only six months after the fuel-injected Vogue had gone on sale, and the engine chosen was a turbocharged four-cylinder VM unit.

It was, we are assured, no more than coincidence that the same basic VM engine had also been chosen for use in the Rover 2400SD Turbo private car. At the time, technical director Bill Morris said:

'High performance diesels offering good levels of pace and economy were relatively easy to find. There were also several units offering very acceptable bottom-end power. But only the VM unit provided the potential to satisfy both requirements – and therefore satisfy a Range Rover customer.'

Sixteen years after its original launch, the Range Rover finally gained a diesel engine option. The power unit chosen was an Italian-built VM four-cylinder unit, complete with KKK turbocharger, and intercooling, which was a comfortable fit in the spacious engine bay. This version was not available on the North American market

Three other manufacturers were considered before agreement was reached with Stabilimenti Meccanici VM of Cento, in Italy, and it took two years before the re-developed engine was ready for use. Although Land-Rover insisted that the 2.4-litre VM diesel was a purpose-designed engine, far removed from the original, there was no doubt about its origin. In the Rover 2400SD Turbo, the engine's capacity was 2,393cc, and its type number was VM HR 492 HT, whereas in the Range Rover it was the same size, considerably more powerful, and carried the type number of VM HR 492 HI.

[This VM engine, incidentally, was clearly very popular, for it also found a home in the Alfa Romeo 90 saloon car of the period, as type number VM 81 A].

The result of this Anglo-Italian collaboration was that the Range Rover Turbo D was given Europe's most powerful four-wheel-drive diesel engine – its peak rating was 112bhp (DIN) at 4,200rpm, with maximum torque of 188lbft at 2,400rpm.

For comparison the Rover 2400SD Turbo figures, for the very similar engine, were 91bhp at 4,200rpm, and 142lbft at 2,350rpm.

Daimler-Benz, for example, already had a choice of diesel engines in its *Geländewagen*, but these were rated at only 72bhp and 88bhp for 2.4-litre and 3.0-litre engines, respectively.

The VM engine was a sturdy and well proven design, which not only featured turbocharging and fuel-injection, but had four separate light-alloy cylinder heads (one per cylinder) and intercooling of the pressurised air down-stream of the KKK turbo itself. In addition, there was a thermostatically controlled engine oil cooler built in to the overall 'envelope' of the high-capacity cooling radiator. There were no changes to the overall gearing, though automatic transmission was not available.

There are, of course, some journalists who make it their business to denigrate anything which is not entirely to their liking, so it was inevitable that one or two of them carped at the VM engine's lack of low-speed torque. Although it was true that there was no turbo effect below 2,000rpm, the new Turbo D model was actually a lively machine, with a claimed top speed of 90mph, and 0–60mph acceleration in around 18 seconds; this, by the way, was equal to the performance offered by *any* of the Range Rover's rivals, with a diesel *or* a petrol engine. The other important statistic, factory-claimed, was a potential of 30mpg cruising economy – and that was a huge increase, up to 100 per cent better, compared with vee-8 engined Range Rovers.

The Turbo D, by its very nature, was expected to sell strongly in mainland Europe, where diesel fuel was much cheaper than petrol –

To prove that the Turbo D version of the Range Rover was as fast as claimed, Land-Rover Ltd used one example to set 27 Class D Endurance records, at up to 24 hours duration

and this automatically ruled out the home market, where prices were closely aligned. Plans were originally laid for up to 3,500 diesel-powered Range Rovers to be built in a full year – up to 20 per cent of production – though the VM engine was not thought likely to account for more than 10 per cent of UK sales.

The Turbo D, in fact, had an entirely different character from the famous vee-8 engined types, for the four-cylinder VM engine was un-avoidably rougher and somewhat 'harder' than this – and at higher speeds it was also significantly more noisy. Land-Rover Ltd, however, were confident of the car's performance, so much so that in September 1986 a lightly-tuned example was taken to the MIRA proving grounds and set to attack a variety of endurance speed records.

This was a complete success. 'Project Bullet', as it was called, involved a team of six drivers and 21 pit crew members, and by using two different vehicles the company was able to set 27 new Diesel Class D records, culminating with an overall average speed of 101.48mph for 24 hours. Incidentally, if you think that fast pit stops are confined to Grand Prix teams, the pit crew on this attempt managed to refuel the 18-gallon tank in a mere 14 seconds, and – where a driver change was also involved – could do the whole thing in 34 seconds!

In the meantime, the company had steadily been working on the most glamorous, and high-risk, project of all. After a great deal of de-

In time for launch in the USA, the Range Rover received a new grille style, concealed bonnet hinges, and many other detail improvements

liberation (and after a lengthy history of dithering under previous management regimes) the company had decided to begin exporting Range Rovers to North America. This was, at one and the same time, the biggest opportunity, and the biggest risk, which the company had faced for many years.

The Range Rover went on sale in the United States in the spring of 1987, nearly 17 years after it had originally been launched, and right from the start it looked as if it could carve out a niche for itself. So, if it was so well received in 1987, why had the launch been delayed for so long?

In the 1970s it had always been clear that a great deal of work would be needed to re-tailor the Range Rover to meet USA legislation. Not only would mountains of safety regulations have to be met (but did anyone doubt that the Range Rover could pass the compulsory crash tests!), but the engine would have to be changed to meet stringent de-toxing legislation. In the early years, and while Range Rover sales were always limited by the ability actually to produce the cars, it never seemed to make commercial sense to tackle this work.

In the early 1980s, however, the tide turned. Not only was Range Rover production being expanded as that of the Land-Rover declined, but experience with the vee-8 engine made its de-toxing a more straightforward task to face. The engine, in fact, had been extensively re-worked by BL Cars for use in the USA-market Triumph TR8 sports car, and the Rover 3500 executive saloon, and the fuel-injection installation developed for these cars was also slated for use in the 1986-model Range Rover Vogue.

The big decision was announced in December 1985 – a new subsidiary company, Range Rover of North America; was being set up; the aim was to appoint up to 60 dealers, deliveries were to begin in 1987, and the target was to sell up to 3,000 vehicles in the first year. It was not before time, for a significant 'grey market' in the import of Range Rovers to the USA had built up in recent years.

It was, nevertheless, a big gamble. Although the reputation of the Range Rover was very high in the United States, but only at long range, that of the name 'Rover' was distinctly tattered. In the last 15 years there had been three different attempts to establish the Rover marque in the US market, and all had failed. The most recent Rover car sold in the United States, the vee-8 engined 3500 saloon, had failed ignominiously. For the Range Rover to succeed, it would have to be sold through an entirely fresh dealer network (not the discredited British Leyland outlets), and it needed to exude supreme product quality.

Range Rover of North America was set up by Charles R. (Charlie) Hughes, who already had two decades of business success with organisations importing marques like Porsche and Ferrari. Right away, he began to choose dealers in the most prosperous areas of the USA – California, Florida, and the classic 'yuppie' areas of New York, Washington, and New England.

Because the USA was already stuffed full of utilitarian 4×4s, like the Jeep Cherokees and Wagoneers, the 1987 Range Rover was marketed as the plushiest-possible 4×4 which an American could buy. Not only was the vehicle based on the latest fuel-injected Vogue chassis (which, nonetheless, had to be de-tuned to 150bhp to meet exhaust emission regulations), but it was given full air-conditioning, four-speed automatic transmission, electric seat adjustments, and a cruise control as standard. It was aimed fairly and squarely at the individual buyer who was earning at least $100,000 a year, and might already have two or three other vehicles in his garage.

Without a doubt, the USA-market Range Rover was always going to be expensive – in mid-1987, as deliveries began in earnest, it was placarded at $31,900 (or about £20,000), and the *only* optional extra was leather upholstery, for another $1,075 – but no-one thought it was over-priced.

Initially there was a rush to buy, with customers putting down deposits in the hope of jumping the queue for deliveries. By mid-1987 the year's allocation had already been sold out, and some dealers were already booking firm orders for a year in advance – and *that*, in 'I want it *now*' North America, was quite amazing.

It was all very encouraging, and Tony Gilroy's colleagues laid plans to increase Range Rover production still further in the late 1980s. But could a car styled in the 1960s, and already on sale for nearly two decades, really make it through into the 1990s without a complete re-design? All the signs were that it could. . . .

USA-market Range Rovers, 1987-style, had automatic transmission and cruise control as standard. Leather seats were the only options in a very comprehensively-equipped package

Appendices

1 Technical Specifications, 1948 to date

Over the years there have been so many variations on the basic Land-Rover theme that I have found it quite impracticable to list every slight difference in tabular form. The specifications which follow are indicative of only the basic Land-Rover types produced between 1948 and the present day.

Unladen weights depend on the type of bodywork used, and the extra items fitted. Since every Land-Rover has a recommended maximum vehicle weight, it follows that heavy versions can carry a less useful payload.

Land-Rover Series I (80in model)—produced 1948 to 1951
Engine: 4-cyl, 69.5 × 105mm, 1,595cc, CR 6.8:1, Solex carb. 50bhp (net) at 4,000rpm. Maximum torque 80lb ft at 2,000rpm.
Transmission: Permanent four-wheel-drive with freewheel in front drive. Front and rear differentials. High and low range of gears. Axle ratios 4.7:1. High range step-down ratio 1.148:1; overall gear ratios 5.396, 8.039, 11.023, 16.165, reverse 13.743:1. Low range step-down ratio 2.89:1; overall ratios 13.578, 20.229, 27.738, 40.676, reverse 34.581:1. Synchromesh on top and third gears.
Suspension and brakes: Live front axle, half-elliptic leaf springs, telescopic dampers; live rear axle, half-elliptic leaf springs, telescopic dampers. Worm and nut steering 10 × 1½in front and rear drum brakes. 6.00–16in or 7.00–16in tyres.
Dimensions: Wheelbase 6ft 8in (80in); front and rear tracks 4ft 2in. Length 11ft 0in; width 5ft 1in; height (hood up) 5ft 10.5in. Unladen weight 2,594lb. Max. payload 1,000lb.

Land-Rover Series I (80in model)—produced 1952 to 1954
Specification as for original 80in model except for:
Engine: 77.8 × 105mm, 1,997cc, CR 6.8:1. 52bhp (net) at 4,000rpm. Maximum torque 101lb ft at 1,500rpm.
Transmission: (Introduced in 1950.) Optional four-wheel or rear-weel drive. No freewheel.
Dimensions: Height (hood up) 6ft 1.5in. Unladen weight 2,604lb.

Land-Rover Series I (86in model)—produced 1954 to 1956
Specification as for previous 80in model except for:
Dimensions: Wheelbase 7ft 2in (86in). Length 11ft 8.7in; width 5ft 2.6in; height (hood up) 6ft 4in. Unladen weight 2,702lb.

Land-Rover Series I (107in model)—produced 1954 to 1958
Specification as for previous 80in model except for:
Dimensions: Wheelbase 8ft 11in (107in). Length 14ft 5.5in; width 5ft 2.6in; height (hood up) 6ft 11.5in. Unladen weight 3,031lb. Max. allowable vehicle weight 4,151lb.

Land-Rover Series I (88in model)—produced 1956 to 1958
Specification as for final 80in model except for:
Dimensions: Wheelbase 7ft 4in (88in). Length 11ft 8.75in; width 5ft 2.6in; height (hood up) 6ft 4in. Unladen weight from 2,740lb. Max. allowable vehicle weight 4,190lb.

Land-Rover Series I (109in model)—produced 1956 to 1958
Specification as for final 80in model except for:
Dimensions: Wheelbase 9ft 1in (109in). Length 14ft 5.5in; width 5ft 2.6in; height (hood up) 6ft 11.5in. Unladen weight 3,080lb. Max. allowable vehicle weight 5,185lb.

Alternative diesel engine, 2,052cc—produced 1957 to 1958
Engine: 85.7 × 88.9mm, 2,052cc, CR 22.5:1, CAV fuel injection. 51bhp (net) at 3,500 rpm. Maximum torque 87lb ft at 2,000rpm.
Dimensions: Extra weight 195lb. Extra max. payload 117lb.

Land-Rover Series II (88in model)—produced 1958 to 1961
Engine: 4-cyl, 90.47 × 88.9mm 2,286cc, CR 7.0:1, Solex carb. 70bhp (net) at 4,250rpm. Maximum torque 124lb ft at 2,500rpm.
Transmission: Optional four-wheel or rear-wheel drive. Front and rear differentials. High and low range of gears. Axle ratios 4.7:1. High range step-down ratio 1.148:1; overall gear ratios 5.396, 7.435, 11.026, 16.171, reverse 13.745:1. 15.1mph/1,000rpm in top gear. Low range step-down ratio 2.888:1; overall ratios 13.578, 18.707, 27.742, 40.688, reverse 34.585:1. 7.3mph/1,000rpm in top gear. Synchromesh on top and 3rd gears.
Suspension and brakes: Live front axle, half-elliptic leaf springs, telescopic dampers; live rear axle, half-elliptic leaf springs, telescopic dampers. Recirculating ball steering. 10 × 1½ front and rear drum brakes. 6.00–16in tyres.
Dimensions: Wheelbase 7ft 4in (88in); front and rear tracks 4ft 3.5in. Length 11ft 10.4in; width 5ft 4in; height (max.) 6ft 5.5in. Unladen weight from 2,900lb. Max. allowable vehicle weight 4,453lb.

Land-Rover Series II (109in model)—produced 1958 to 1961
Specification as for 88in model except for:
Suspension and brakes: 11 × 2¼ front and rear brakes, 7.50–16in tyres.
Dimensions: Wheelbase 9ft 1in (109in). Length 14ft 7in; height (max.) 6ft 9in. Unladen weight from 3,294lb. Max. allowable vehicle weight 5,905lb.

Alternative diesel engine, 2,052cc—produced 1958 to 1961
Engine : 85.7 × 88.9mm, 2,052cc CR 22.5: 1, CAV fuel injection. 51bhp (net) at 3,500rpm. Maximum torque 87lb ft at 2,000rpm.
Dimensions: Extra weight 195lb. Extra max. payload 117lb.

Land-Rover Series IIA (88in model)—produced 1961 to 1971
Specification as for Series II 88in model except for:
Dimensions: Unladen weight, from 2,953lb. Max. allowable vehicle weight 4,453lb.

Land-Rover Series IIA (109in model)—produced 1961 to 1971
Specification as for Series II 109in model except for:
Dimensions: Unladen weight from 3,301lb. Max. allowable vehicle weight 5,905lb.

Alternative Series IIA diesel engine, 2,286cc—produced 1961 to 1971
Engine: 90.47 × 88.9mm, 2,286cc, CR 23.0: 1 CAV fuel injection. 62bhp at 4,000 rpm. Maximum torque 103lb ft at 1,800rpm.
Dimensions: Extra weight 144lb. Extra max. payload 168lb.

Land-Rover Series IIA (109in 6-cyl model)—produced 1967 to 1971
Specification as for normal Series II/Series IIA 109in petrol model except for:
Engine: 6-cyl, 77.8 × 92.1mm, 2,625cc, CR 7.8:1, SU carb. 83bhp (net) at 4,500rpm. Maximum torque 128lb ft at 1,500rpm.
*Transmission: High range step-down ratio 1.148: 1; overall gear ratios 5.396, 8.09, 11.98, 19.43, reverse 16.30: 1. 16.5mph/1,000rpm in top gear. Low range step-down ratio 2.35: 1; overall ratios 11.04, 16.57, 24.51, 39.74, reverse 33.34: 1. 8.0mph/1,000rpm in top gear.
Suspension and brakes: Front brakes 11 × 3in drums.
Dimensions: : Unladen weight from 3,459lb. Max. allowable vehicle weight 5,905lb.

*Note, these gearbox ratios standardised for all normal-control Land-Rovers once the six-cylinder version was introduced.

Land-Rover Series IIA (109in '1 ton' model)—produced 1968 to 1971
Specification as for normal Series IIA 109in model except for:
Transmission: High range step-down ratio 1.53: 1; overall gear ratios 7.19, 10.80, 15.96, 25.90, reverse 21.7: 1. 13.3mph/1,000rpm in top gear. Low range step-down ratio 3.27: 1; overall ratios 15.40, 23.10, 34.10, 55.3, reverse 46.4: 1. 6.25mph/1,000rpm in top gear.
Suspension and brakes: 9.00–16in tyres.
Dimensions: Unladen weight from 3,886lb. Max. allowable vehicle weight 6,750lb.

'Half-ton' Military Land-Rover (88in model)—produced 1968 to date
Specification as for appropriately engined (four-cylinder, petrol or diesel)
Series IIA or Series III civil Land-Rovers except for:
Dimensions: Length 12ft 0in; width 5ft 0in; height 6ft 5in. Unladen weight
(petrol engine) 3,210lb; in stripped-out form for air transportation, 2,660lb.
Max. allowable vehicle weight 4,450lb.

Land-Rover Series III (88 model)—produced 1971 to 1985
Engine: 4-cyl, 90.47 × 88.9mm, 2,286cc, CR 8.0:1, Zenith carb. 70bhp
(DIN) at 4,000rpm. Maximum torque 120lb ft at 1,500rpm.
Transmission: Optional four-wheel or rear-wheel drive. Front and rear
differentials. High and low range of gears. Axle ratios 4.7:1. High range
step-down ratios 1.148:1. All synchromesh gearbox, overall gear ratios
5.396, 8.05, 12.00, 19.88, reverse 21.66:1. 15.1mph/1,000rpm in top gear.
Low range step-down ratio 2.35:1; overall ratios 11.10, 16.50, 24.60, 40.70,
reverse 44.30:1. 7.4mph/1,000rpm in top gear.
Suspension and brakes: Live front axle, half-elliptic leaf springs, telescopic
dampers; live rear axle, half-elliptic leaf springs, telescopic dampers.
Recirculating ball steering. 10 × 1½in front and rear drum brakes. 6.00–16in
tyres.
Dimensions: Wheelbase 7ft 4in (88in); front and rear tracks 4ft 3.5in.
Length 11ft 10.6in; width 5ft 6in; height (max.) 6ft 5in. Unladen weight
from 2,953lb. Max. allowable vehicle weight 4,453lb.

Land-Rover Series III (109in model)—produced 1971 to 1985
Specification as for 88in model except for:
Transmission: 16.5mph/1,000rpm in high range; 8.0mph/1,000rpm in low
range.
Suspension and brakes: 11 × 2¼in front and rear drum brakes. 7.50–16in
tyres.
Dimensions: Wheelbase 9ft 1in (109in); front and rear tracks 4ft 4.5in.
Length 14ft 7in; height (max.) 6ft 7in. Unladen weight from 3,301lb. Max.
allowable vehicle weight 5,905lb.

Land-Rover Series III (109in, 6-cyl model)—produced 1971 to 1985
Specification as for normal Series III 109in model except for:
Engine: 6-cyl, 77.8 × 92.1mm, 2,625cc, CR 7.8:1, Zenith-Stromberg carb.
86bhp (DIN) at 4,500rpm. Maximum torque 132lb ft at 1,500rpm.
Dimensions: Unladen weight from 3,459lb. Max. allowable vehicle weight
5,905lb.

Alternative Series III diesel engine, 2,286cc—produced 1971 to 1985
Engine: 90.47 × 88.9mm, 2,286cc; CR 23.0:1, CAV fuel injection. 62bhp
(DIN) at 4,000rpm. Maximum torque 103lb ft at 1,800rpm.
Dimensions: Extra weight 144lb. Extra allowed max. vehicle weight 312lb.

Land-Rover Series III (109in '1 ton' model)—produced 1971 to 1985
Specification as for normal Series III 109in model except for:
Transmission: High range step-down ratio 1.53: 1; overall gear ratios 7.19, 10.80, 15.96, 26.46, reverse 28.91: 1. 13.3mph/1,000rpm in top gear. Low range step-down ratio 3.27: 1; overall ratios 15.40, 23.10, 34.10, 56.56, reverse 61.78: 1. 6.25mph/1,000rpm in top gear. 9.00–16in tyres.
Dimensions: Unladen weight from 3,886lb Max. allowable vehicle weight 6,750lb.

Land-Rover Forward-Control (109in)—produced 1962 to 1966
Engine: 4-cyl, 90.47 × 88.9mm, 2,286cc, CR 7.0: 1, Solex carb, 67bhp (net) at 4,000rpm. Maximum torque 116lb ft at 1,500rpm.
Transmission: Optional four-wheel or rear-wheel drive. Front and rear differentials. High and low range of gears. Axle ratios 4.7: 1. High range step-down ratio 1.53: 1; overall gear ratios 7.19, 10.86, 15.96, 25.90, reverse 21.7: 1. 13.3mph/1,000rpm in top gear. Low range step-down ratio 2.92: 1; overall ratios 13.72, 20.7, 30.5, 49.4, reverse 41.4: 1. 7.0mph/1,000rpm in top gear.
Suspension and brakes: Live front axle, half-elliptic leaf springs, telescopic dampers; live rear axle, half-elliptic leaf springs, telescopic dampers. Recirculating ball steering. 11 × 3in front and 11 × 2¼in rear drum brakes, with servo assistance. 9.00–16in tyres.
Dimensions: Wheelbase 9ft 1in (109in); front and rear tracks 4ft 5.5in. Length 16ft 1in; width 6ft 3.5in; height (max.) 8ft 6in. Unladen weight from 4,200lb. Max. allowable vehicle weight 8,000lb.

Land-Rover Forward-Control (110in)—produced 1966 to 1972
Specification as for 109in Forward-Control model except for:
Transmission: High range step-down ratio 1.53: 1 as before. Low range step-down ratio 3.27: 1; overall low range ratios 15.4, 23.1, 34.1, 55.3, reverse 46.4: 1. 6.25mph/1,000rpm in top gear. Front suspension had an anti-roll bar.
Dimensions: Wheelbase 9ft 2in (110in); front and rear tracks 4ft 9.5in. Length 16ft 1in; width 6ft 3.5in; height (max.) 8ft 6in. Unladen weight from 4,341lb. Max. allowable vehicle weight 8,250lb.

In addition, this model was available with the diesel engine, and 6-cyl, 2,625cc petrol engine alternatives. The unladen weight with the 'six' was not changed. For the diesel, the unladen weight became 4,505lb. Max. allowable vehicle weight remained the same.

Range Rover—produced 1970 to date
Engine: V8-cyl, 88.9 × 71.1mm, 3,528cc, CR 8.5: 1, 2 Zenith-Stromberg CD2 carbs. 135bhp (DIN) at 4,750rpm. Maximum torque 205lb ft at 3,000rpm.
Transmission: Permanent four-wheel drive, three differentials, high and low range of gears. Axle ratios 3.54: 1. High range step-down ratio 1.174: 1; all synchromesh gearbox; overall ratios 4.16, 6.25, 10.17, 16.91, reverse 15.23: 1. 20.0mph/1,000rpm in top gear. Low range step-down ratio 3.321: 1; overall ratios 11.76, 17.69, 28.78, 47.84, reverse 43.07: 1. 7.07mph/1,000rpm in top gear.

Suspension and brakes: Live front axle, coil springs, radius arms, Panhard rod, telescopic dampers; live rear axle, coil springs, radius arms, A-bracket, telescopic dampers, self-levelling strut. Recirculating ball steering. 11.8in front disc brakes, 11.4in rear disc brakes. 205–16in tyres on 6.0in rims.

Dimensions: Wheelbase 8ft 4in; front track 4ft 10.5in; rear track 4ft 10.5in. Length 14ft 8in; width 5ft 10in; height 5ft 10in. Unladen weight (approx) 3,880lb.

Power assisted steering became optional in January 1973 (at Chassis No 5287).

From Autumn 1976 the high range step-down ratio became 1.116:1, and overall gear ratios became 3.95, 5.95, 9.80, 16.07, reverse 14.48:1. Low range was not affected. 21.1mph/1,000rpm in top gear.

Fairey overdrive became optional in 1978, with step-up ratio of 0.782, operating on all forward gears. O/d top gear (high range) is 3.09:1. 27.02mph/1,000rpm in o/d top gear.

From July 1981, engine retuned as follows: CR 9.35:1. 125bhp (DIN) at 4,000rpm. Maximum torque 185lb ft at 2,500rpm. High range step-down ratio 0.996:1, overall ratios 3.525, 5.32, 8.64, 14.35, reverse 12.92:1. Low ratio was not affected. 23.7mph/1,000rpm in top gear.

From August 1982, automatic transmission became optional, by Chrysler Torqueflite A727 unit. Transfer box ratios: 1.003:1 (high range), 3.32:1 (low range). Overall ratios: (high range) 3.55, 5.15, 8.70, reverse 7.81, (low range) 11.75, 17.04, 28.79, reverse 25.85:1. Stall torque ratio (max) 1.94:1.

From July 1983, five speed transmission, with all synchromesh on forward gears, was fitted. Final drive ratio 3.54:1. Transfer box ratios 1.192:1 (high range), 3.32:1 (low range). Overall ratios: (high range) 3.25, 4.22, 5.91, 8.99, 14.01, reverse 14.47:1. 25.8mph/1000rpm in fifth gear. (Low range) 9.05, 11.75, 16.45, 25.03, 39.01, reverse 40.30:1. 9.26mph/1000rpm in fifth gear.

From October 1985, fuel-injected 165bhp engine on Vogue models and new four-speed ZF automatic transmission option, all models. Details as follows:

Vogue engine: Lucas 'L' electronic fuel injection, 165bhp (DIN) at 4,750rpm. Maximum torque 206lbft at 3,200rpm. Carburettor engine now re-rated at 127bhp (DIN) at 4,000rpm. Maximum torque 194lbft at 2,500rpm.

Transmission: Manual transmission as before, optional ZF 4HP22 automatic transmission unit. Transfer box ratios 1.19:1 (high range), 3.32:1 (low range).

Overall automatic transmission ratios: (high range) 3.04, 4.22, 6.20, 10.42, reverse 8.78:1; 30.1mph/1,000rpm in fourth ratio.

Tyres: Optional, 215/75–16in. Avon Rangemaster or 205–16 Michelin XM+S 200 on Vogue model.

From April 1986, Range Rover Turbo D model announced, featuring VM turbo-charged diesel engine. Four-cylinder engine, 92 × 90mm, 2,393cc, CR 22.0:1, KKK turbocharger, with indirect fuel injection. 112bhp (DIN) at 4,200rpm. Maximum torque 183lbft at 2,400rpm.

From December 1986, 165bhp fuel-injected engine standardised on all 4-

door models (except USA-spec. model). Transfer box high-range ratio now 1.22:1.

Spring 1987, Range Rover introduced to USA market. Basically as for UK-spec. Vogue model, except for: 150bhp (DIN) at 4,750rpm. Maximum torque 195lbft at 3,000rpm.

101in Forward-Control Military Land-Rover—produced 1975 to 1978
Engine: V8-cyl, 88.9 × 71.1mm, 3,528cc, CR 8.5:1, 2 Zenith-Stromberg carbs. 135bhp (DIN) at 4,750rpm. Maximum torque 205lb ft at 3,000rpm.
Transmission: Permanent four-wheel drive, three differentials, high and low range of gears. Axle ratios 5.57:1. High range step-down ratio 1.174:1; overall gear ratios 6.54, 9.84, 16.01, 26.55, reverse 23.97:1. Low range step-down ratio 3.321:1; overall ratios 18.50, 27.84, 45.29, 75.11, reverse 67.80:1.
Suspension and brakes: Live front axle, half-elliptic leaf springs, telescopic dampers; live rear axle, half-elliptic leaf springs, telescopic dampers. Recirculating ball steering. Drum brakes at front and rear, servo-assisted. 9.00–15in tyres on 6.5in rims.
Dimensions: Wheelbase 8ft 5in; front track 5ft 0in; rear track 5ft 1in. Length 13ft 6.5in; width 6ft 0.5in; height 7ft 4in. Unladen weight (approx) 4,040lb. Max. payload 2,204lb.

109in V8-engined Land-Rover—introduced 1979
Engine: V8-cyl, 88.9 × 71.1mm, 3,528cc, CR 8.1:1, 2 Zenith-Stromberg carbs. 91bhp (DIN) at 3,500rpm. Maximum torque 166lb ft at 2,000rpm.
Transmission: Permanent four-wheel drive, three differentials, high and low range of gears. Axle ratios 3.54:1. High range step-down ratio 1.336:1; overall gear ratios 4.73, 7.12, 11.57, 19.24, reverse 17.33:1. 18.82mph/1,000rpm in top gear. Low range step-down ratio 3.321:1; overall ratios 11.75, 17.68, 28.76, 47.81, reverse 43.05:1. 7.56mph/1,000rpm in top gear.
Suspension and brakes: Live front axle, half-elliptic leaf springs, telescopic dampers; live rear axle, half-elliptic leaf springs, telescopic dampers. Recirculating ball steering. 11 × 3in front and 11 × 2¼in rear drum brakes, with servo-assistance. 7.50–16in tyres.
Dimensions: Wheelbase 9ft 1in (109in); front and rear tracks 4ft 4.5in. Length 14ft 9in; height (max.) 6ft 7in; width 5ft 6in. Unladen weight from 3,396lb. Max. allowable vehicle weight 5,976lb.

Land-Rover One-Ten—introduced 1983
Engines: 4-cyl petrol, 90.47 x 88.9mm, 2,286cc, CR 8.0:1, Weber carb. 74bhp (DIN) at 4,000rpm. Maximum torque 120lb ft at 2,000rpm.
4-cyl Diesel, 90.47 x 88.9mm, 2,286cc, CR 23.0:1, CAV fuel injection. 60bhp (DIN) at 4,000rpm. Maximum torque 103lb ft at 1,800rpm.
V8-cyl petrol, 88.9 x 71.1mm, 3,528cc. CR 8.13:1, 2 Zenith-Stromberg 175 CDSE carbs. 114bhp (DIN) at 4,000rpm. Maximum torque 185lb ft at 2,500rpm.

Transmission: Permanent four-wheel drive, three differentials, high and low range of gears. Axle ratios, all derivatives, 3.54:1. 4-cyl cars: High range step-down ratio 1.66:1; overall gear ratios (five forward ratios) 4.90, 5.89, 8.89, 13.57, 21.14, reverse 21.82:1. Low range step-down ratio 3.31:1; overall gear ratios (five forward ratios) 9.76, 11.74, 17.70, 27.02, 42.11, reverse 43.47:1. V8-cyl cars: High range step-down ·ratio 1.34:1; overall gear ratios (four forward ratios) 4.72, 7.11, 11.57, 19.23, reverse 17.32:1. Low range step-down ratio 3.32:1; overall gear ratios (four forward ratios) 11.74, 17.68, 28.76, 47.81, reverse 43.05:1.

Suspension and brakes: Live front axle, coil springs, radius arms, Panhard rod, telescopic dampers; live rear axle, coil springs, radius arms, A-bracket, optional self-levelling (standard on 'County' station wagons), and telescopic dampers. Recirculating ball steering, optional power-assistance. 11.8in front disc brakes, 11.0in rear drum brakes, with vacuum servo assistance. 7.50–16in tyres on 5.5in rims.

Dimensions: Wheelbase 9ft 2in (110in); front and rear tracks 4ft 10.5in. Length 14ft 7in; height 6ft 8.1in; width 5ft 10.5in. Unladen weight from 3,799lb. Max. allowable vehicle weight 6,724lb, or 6,504lb with self-levelling suspension.

From January 1984, an enlarged diesel (but not petrol) engine was fitted: 90.47 x 97mm, 2,495cc, CR 21.0:1, DPS fuel injection. 67bhp (DIN) at 4,000rpm. Maximum torque 114lb ft at 1,800rpm.

From May 1985, a new five speed all-synchromesh gearbox (type LT85) was fitted ·to the V8-engined derivatives: High range step-down ratio 1.410:1; overall gear ratios (five forward ratios) 3.97, 4.99, 7.165, 10.88, 18.22, reverse 19.085:1. Low range step-down ratio 3.32:1; overall gear ratios (five forward ratios) 9.34, 11.75, 16.87, 25.61, 42.99, reverse 44.93:1.

From August 1985, the four-cylinder petrol engine was also enlarged to 2,495cc (bore and stroke as for Diesel engine). 83bhp (DIN) at 4,000rpm. Maximum torque 133lbft at 2,000rpm.

From October 1986, a turbocharged version of the 2,495cc diesel engine was introduced: 85bhp (DIN) at 4,000rpm. Maximum torque 150lbft at 1,800rpm. Garrett AiResearch T2 turbocharger, with DPS fuel injection system. Transmission: High range step-down ratio 1.411:1. Low range step-down ratio 3.32:1. Same five-speed main gearbox as before.

From October 1986, a more powerful version of the optional vee-8 engine was phased in: 134bhp (DIN) at 5,000rpm. Maximum torque 187lbft at 2,500rpm. Transmission: High range step-down gear ratio 1.222:1. Low-range step-down ratio 3.32:1. Same five-speed main gearbox as before.

Land-Rover Ninety—introduced 1984

Engines: 4-cyl petrol as One-Ten, 4-cyl Diesel as 2.5-litre 1984 One-Ten, V8-cyl engines (from May 1985 only) as One-Ten.

Transmission: Permanent four-wheel drive as One-Ten, but: 4-cyl cars: High range step-down ratio 1.41:1; overall gear ratios (five forward ratios), 4.14, 4.99, 7.52, 11.49, 17.91, reverse 18.46:1. Low range as One-Ten.

V8-cyl cars (from May 1985 only): High range step-down ratio 1.19:1;

overall gear ratios (five forward ratios), 3.355, 4.22, 6.06, 9.20, 15.40, reverse 16.14: 1. Low range step-down ratio 3.32: 1, overall ratios as for V8-cyl five-speed One-Ten.

Suspension and brakes: As One-Ten, except tyres 6.00–16in (County: 205–16in).

Dimensions: Wheelbase 7ft 8.9in. (92.9in); front and rear tracks 4ft 10.5in. Length 12ft 2.5in; height 6ft 5.6in (max); width 5ft 10.5in. Unladen weight from 3,540lb. Max. allowable vehicle weight 5,513lb.

From October 1986 (as for Land-Rover One-Ten), turbocharged four-cylinder 2,495cc diesel engine option, and up-rated (134bhp) vee-8 engines became standard. Transmission: High ratio step-down gear ratio (turbo-diesel and 1987-model vee-8 engined models) 1.411:1. Low range step-down ratio (turbo-diesel and 1987-model vee-8 engined models) 3.32:1. Same five-speed main gearbox as before.

2 Major Development Milestones

Spring 1947
Land-Rover project began. Jeep design studied closely at first. Original prototype used Jeep chassis and other components. First prototype completed in early summer 1947.

Autumn 1947/early 1948
First twenty-five 'pilot' Land-Rovers built, for test, assessment and proving purposes.

April 1948
Vehicle first shown publicly on 30 April at the Amsterdam motor show, and technical analyses appeared in British motoring press. Only one version announced at this stage—with 80in wheelbase, pick-up body and 1,595cc Rover 'P3' type of 4-cyl. engine Permanent four-wheel drive and freewheel in front drive line. Provisional British price £450, with very sparse equipment.

July 1948
'Pilot-run' production ended at total of forty-eight machines. True volume production began this month. Price £450 with better fittings.

October 1948
First body variant revealed; light-alloy panelled station wagon, which qualified (in Britain) as a private car and attracted purchase tax. Total price £959. Built until early 1951.

1950
Metal 'van' top offered for the first time as an alternative to the canvas hood. Freewheel feature discontinued. Transmission now had optional four-wheel or rear-wheel drive with cockpit control.

1952
From beginning of the year the engine was changed. The much-modified 1,997cc i.o.e.v. unit replaced the original 1,595cc unit with no overlap period.

1954
Wheelbase of original Land-Rover increased from 80in to 86in (and a total increase in overall length of 9in). At the same time a long-wheelbase (107in) version, with extra 41in length of loading platform compared with original 80in machine.

October 1956
Each basic version given new chassis with extra 2in in wheelbase—to 88in and 109in respectively. Extra space in engine bay to accommodate new diesel and petrol engines, not yet ready for announcement. No increase in carrying capacity. The 88in and 109in dimensions have been standard ever since. To balance supply situation of components, 107in station wagon was to continue until September 1958.

June 1957
Announcement of diesel engine option for first time. An all-new engine, of 2,052cc, with overhead valves, entirely different from existing Land-Rover petrol unit. Available at once in British-market machines, on export after a few months, in 88in or 109in versions.

April 1958
Series II Land-Rover replaced all existing Series I models (except—for a few months—for the 107in station wagon). Chassis virtually unchanged, but wheel tracks increased, available front wheel lock increased, and turning circles reduced (by 5ft on 109in models). New styling features, including 'barrel' body sides, and covering panels at side. Original 1,997cc engine announced as discontinued, but actually persisted in some versions until the autumn of 1958. New overhead valve engine of 2,286cc announced, sharing many common parts and much common engineering and production tooling with the diesel engine.

November 1959
250,000th Land-Rover completed—more than 11 years after the machine went into production.

September 1961
Series IIA Land-Rovers replace Series II Land-Rovers. Principal mechanical change was to enlarge the diesel engine to 2,286cc, thus commonising the bore and stroke with the petrol engine.

September 1962
Announcement of forward-control Land-Rover, which used 75 per cent of existing 109in chassis components. Frame based on existing 109in frame, with a complete new overframe, raised and much-altered cab, and a 30cwt (1,525kg) payload, or 25cwt (1,270kg) when driving across rough country. The 2,286cc petrol engine was standardised on this model, for power/ weight reasons, with no diesel option.

April 1966
500,000th Land-Rover completed at Solihull—6½years after 250,000th.

September 1966
Wheelbase of forward-control machine changed to 110in by minor modifi-

cation to suspensions. Choice of three engines in this model—2,286cc petrol, 2,286cc diesel, and 2,625cc six-cylinder petrol engine. The 'six' had not been offered on Land-Rovers before this occasion. In design it was related both to 1,595cc/1,997cc Land-Rover engines of 1948–58, and to current P5 Rover saloon units. The 2,286cc petrol engine was not available on British-market examples. Wheeltracks were increased by 4in to improve stability and roadholding.

April 1967
The 2,625cc six-cylinder engine became available on 109in chassis normal-control Series IIA Land-Rovers.

Summer 1967
A 'luxury pack' of three deeply-padded front seats became optional on all normal-control Series IIA Land-Rovers.

Spring 1968
To satisfy certain new legal requirements in export territories (British legislation followed at a later date) the Series IIA Land-Rover's headlamps were moved from their grille-mounted position to the front wings. Apart from slight changes to the front grille this was the first obvious change in Land-Rover styling since 1948.

September 1968
Special heavy-duty '1 ton' version of 109in chassis made available, only with six-cylinder 2,625cc engine. New military version of the 88in Land-Rover was unveiled. Called the '½-ton' (or 'Rover 1' by the British armed forces) which denoted its total payload, it had a standard chassis, but an entirely different lightweight body, which could be stripped out so that the machine could be transported in an aeroplane, or slung underneath a helicopter. This model has never been available to the general public as a new Land-Rover.

February 1969
Headlamps moved to wings on all models.

June 1970
Launch of entirely new Range Rover, related to the Land-Rover, and under the care of the Land-Rover engineers, but mechanically very different. Features included a 100in wheelbase, permanent four-wheel drive, three differentials, light-alloy 3,528cc vee-8 engine, and three-door estate car body with no options.

June 1971
Completion of 750,000th Land-Rover, 5 years after 500,000th example.

October 1971
Announcement of Series III Land-Rovers, replacing the Series IIA range of

normal-control machines. Forward-control Land-Rovers continued as Series IIA types. Series III models mechanically similar to Series IIAs but with new all-synchromesh gearbox (in place of unsynchronised first and second gears). New front grille and details, new full-width facia style and added comfort, with instruments ahead of the driver instead of centrally-mounted. The 88in and 109in wheelbases as before, with continued choice of 2,286cc petrol and diesel engines, and six-cylinder 2,625cc petrol engine.

September 1972
Debut at Commercial Vehicle Show in London of new and specialised forward-control military Land-Rover—the 101in wheelbase machine. Production began in 1974–75, and was confined to vehicles for the British armed forces. It used the Range Rover's vee-8 3,528cc engine and permanent four-wheel drive central transmission, in a new chassis. Simple forward-control cab and pick-up body was provided, and there was a rear power take-off drive allowing the latest Rubery Owen powered trailers to be hitched up, which provided a 6 × 6 combination. It was announced that production of the 'civilian' forward-control Land-Rovers would cease when the last export contract was complete in 1973.

August 1974
Announcement of optional (Fairey) overdrive for Land-Rovers of all types, which attaches to the main gearbox.

June 1976
Production of the one millionth Land-Rover—5 years after the 750,000th machine—which immediately joined the Leyland Historic Vehicles Collection, in company with R.01, the original pilot-production Land-Rover of 1947–8.

1976 and 1977
Plans announced for the doubling of Land-Rover and Range Rover production, based at Solihull, but implementation delayed by British Leyland's financial problems.

February 1978
Announcement of optional Fairey overdrive for the Range Rover, which attaches to the main transfer gearbox.

August/November 1978
Announcement and final approval of plan to double Land-Rover and Range Rover production by early 1980s, at an investment cost of at least £280 million.

March 1979
Announcement of Land-Rover with vee-8 engine. This was merely the first of several important developments planned under the expansion programme.

July 1981
Announcement of four-door Range Rover. £85 million/one million sq ft North Block rebuilding complete – Range Rover assembly, and four-cylinder engine machining and assembly concentrated there.

Early 1982
All car manufacture at Solihull ceased. 'SD1' plant mothballed until 1984.

August 1982
Automatic transmission (Chrysler Torqueflite) made available for Range Rover.

March 1983
Announcement of new generation Land-Rover One-Ten, with coil spring suspension, and 110in wheelbase. Five speed all-synchromesh gearbox on four-cylinder models. V8 version with Range Rover transmission also available.

July 1983
Range Rover now fitted with five speed all-synchromesh type gearbox instead of four-speed.

January 1984
Introduction of 2,495cc diesel four-cylinder engine, directly replacing 2,286cc type – all relevant models.

June 1984
Introduction of new generation Land-Rover Ninety, with shortened version of One-Ten chassis, and coil spring suspension – but wheelbase actually 92.9in! Available only with four-cylinder engines, and with five speed all-synchromesh gearbox.
   Important Range Rover facelift, including new facia style, one-piece front door side windows.

May 1985
Launch of five speed all-synchromesh Spanish-built 'Santana' manual gearbox for V8-engined Land-Rovers; at the same time, V8 engine made available for the first time on the Ninety model. Series III assembly ended a few weeks later.

September 1985
Introduction of 2,495cc petrol four-cylinder engine, directly replacing 2,286cc type – all relevant models.

October 1985
Range Rover Vogue models feature 165bhp V8 fuel injected engine – incorporating the Lucas 'L' electronic fuel injection system.

Automatic ZF4 HP22 four-speed gearbox replaces the Chrysler three-speed originally fitted. Many improvements to both interior and exterior, including new paint process.

October 1985
Completion of the 1,500,000th vehicle off the production lines at Solihull.

April 1986
Launch of Range Rover Turbo D (diesel-engined) model.

June 1986
First showing of new-generation forward-control Land Rover, with vee-8 engine, and five-speed manual gearbox. No definite production plans released at this time.

October 1986
Introduction of 85bhp turbocharged version of existing 2.5-litre diesel engine, optional for all Land-Rovers.

December 1986
Changes to Range Rover for 1987 include new grille, concealed bonnet hinges. All four-door Range Rovers now to be fitted with 165bhp fuel-injected engine.

3 Year by Year Sales, 1948 to date

Land-Rover and Range Rover sales, by financial year, are detailed below. These include all vehicles shipped abroad as CKD packs, but not those built by MSA in Spain.

Up to and including 1973–4, Rover's financial year ran from 1 September to 31 August. In 1974–5 it ran from 1 September 1974 to 26 September 1975. In 1975–6 it ran for 15 months, from 27 September 1975 to 31 December 1976. The 1977 figures represent the complete calendar year, as do all subsequent statistics.

Table 1
Land-Rover

	Annual sales	Cumulative Sales		Annual sales	Cumulative Sales
1947–8	48	48	1967–8	44,928	606,016
1948–9	8,000	8,048	1968–9	50,561	656,577
1949–50	16,085	24,133	1969–70	47,538	704,115
1950–1	17,360	41,493	1970–1	56,663	760,778
1951–2	19,591	61,084	1971–2	52,445	813,223
1952–3	18,570	79,654	1972–3	49,724	862,947
1953–4	20,135	99,789	1973–4	45,169	908,116
1954–5	28,882	128,671	1974–5*	54,298	962,414
1955–6	28,365	157,036	1975–6	58,523	1,020,937
1956–7	25,775	182,811	1977	41,452	1,062,389
1957–8	28,656	211,467	1978	46,172	1,108,561
1958–9	28,371	239,838	1979	42,936	1,151,497
1959–60	34,168	274,006	1980	51,198	1,202,695
1960–1	35,148	309,154	1981	41,059	1,243,754
1961–2	37,139	346,293	1982	38,926	1,282,680
1962–3	34,304	380,597	1983	28,586	1,311,266
1963–4	42,569	423,166	1984	25,562	1,336,828
1964–5	45,790	468,956	1985	31,046	1,367,874
1965–6	47,941	516,897	1986	22,026	1,389,900
1966–7	44,191	561,088			

The first Land-Rover (one of the pilot-run models built before series production commenced) was delivered in July 1948. The quarter million mark was reached in November 1959, more than 11 years after the vehicle's launch. The half-millionth Land-Rover followed in April 1966, the second quarter million being built in 6½ years. The 750,000th Land-Rover was built in June 1971, a little over 5 years after the half-millionth. The millionth machine was built in June 1976.

Table 2
Range Rover

	Annual sales	Cumulative sales		Annual sales	Cumulative sales
1969–70	86	86	1979	11,373	78,259
1970–1	2,537	2,623	1980	9,708	87,967
1971–2	5,510	8,133	1981	10,441	98,408
1972–3	6,519	14,652	1982	13,255	111,663
1973–4	8,604	23,256	1983	12,182	123,845
1974–5	10,516	33,772	1984	11,885	135,730
1975–6	12,207	45,979	1985	13,458	149,188
1977	9,667	55,646	1986	14,495	163,683
1978	11,240	66,886			

Sales—at home and abroad to 1981

The Land-Rover was originally intended to sell well in export markets, and ever since 1948 it has proved to be a great success overseas. Almost three-quarters of all 4 × 4 Rover products have been exported. Sales figures corrected to the end of calendar year 1981 are as follows:

Total number of Land-Rovers built	1,247,000
Home sales (17 per cent)	217,000
Sales to British Government (8 per cent)	93,000
Export sales (75 per cent)	937,000

For the Range Rover, comparative figures are as follows:

Total number of Range Rovers built	98,000
Home sales (25.5 per cent)	25,000
Export sales (74.5 per cent)	73,000

Land-Rovers have sold all over the world. Recently it was estimated that examples had been delivered to every country with the exception of Albania and North Vietnam. The following table gives the 'league table' of countries buying the most for each calendar year from 1964 to 1977 inclusive:

Table 3
Land-Rover exports—best twenty countries

1964		1965		1966	
Australia	4,161	Australia	3,099	Australia	2,685
S. Africa	1,839	S. Africa	2,371	Fr W. & Eq A	1,695
Fr W. & Eq A	1,159	USA	1,840	S. Africa	1,462
East Africa	1,116	Fr W. & Eq A	1,392	PWA	1,304
Switzerland	1,012	Malaysia	1,267	Iran	1,252
USA	952	New Zealand	1,125	New Zealand	1,220
New Zealand	919	East Africa	1,117	USA	1,137
PWA (Port W.		Zambia	980	Libya	1,136
Africa)	891	Switzerland	912	Thailand	1,061
Malaysia	858	PWA	837	Zambia	1,037
Persian Gulf	722	Rhodesia	706	Tanzania	947
Thailand	694	Persian Gulf	680	Nigeria	912
Chile	669	Jordan	661	Persian Gulf	795
S. Rhodesia	655	Thailand	653	East Africa	759
Nigeria	654	Germany	645	Saudi Arabia	589
Libya	599	Algeria	613	Malaysia	586
Saudi Arabia	525	Tanzania	589	Canada	503
Algeria	519	China	575	Sudan	458
Persia (Iran)	477	Nigeria	574	Switzerland	450
Aden (inc Yemen)	428	Libya	552	Iraq	416
Lebanon	377				

1967		1968		1969	
Australia	4,166	S. Africa	3,638	Australia	5,005
S. Africa	2,323	Australia	3,600	S. Africa	2,327
Zambia	1,426	Fr W. & Eq A	1,709	Persian Gulf	2,026
Tanzania	1,309	Persian Gulf	1,523	Fr W. & Eq A	1,907
Nigeria	1,129	Nigeria	1,416	Tanzania	1,426
Persian Gulf	1,122	Tanzania	1,300	Iran	1,423
Thailand	1,096	Zambia	1,200	Nigeria	1,272
CNF	1,093	Libya	1,016	USA	1,222
PWA	941	Thailand	878	Malaysia	1,218
East Africa	794	Angola (ex-PWA)	822	Angola	1,052
New Zealand	715	Congo	790	Libya	1,046
Libya	686	Malaysia	726	Zambia	981
Switzerland	649	Jugoslavia	659	New Zealand	888
Malaysia	573	Morocco	626	Thailand	836
Port E. Africa	495	Saudi Arabia	616	Indonesia	790
Sudan	481	Ghana	612	Sudan	756
Jugoslavia	458	Algeria	553	Jugoslavia	726
Rep Cameroon	422	Kenya	550	Costa Rica	692
USA	415	Switzerland	544	Switzerland	655
Ethiopia	365	Iran	542	Algeria	558

1970		1971		1972	
S. Africa	3,320	S. Africa	3,153	Iran	3,051
Australia	3,296	Australia	3,060	Australia	2,826
Tanzania	1,618	Zambia	2,902	Nigeria	1,707
Iran	1,573	Iran	2,188	Malaysia	1,573
Malaysia	1,440	Tanzania	1,981	S. Africa	1,289
New Zealand	1,382	Nigeria	1,899	Tanzania	1,276
Nigeria	1,363	Malaysia	1,436	Libya	1,146
Zambia	1,301	New Zealand	1,249	USA	1,114
Kinshasa	1,110	Kinshasa	990	Switzerland	844
Angola	1,056	Switzerland	906	Angola	794
USA	873	Angola	826	Algeria	782
Switzerland	861	USA	756	Dubai	738
Costa Rica	798	Cameroon	724	Sudan	716
Venezuela	588	Ghana	720	Portugal	691
Thailand	570	Costa Rica	673	Singapore	676
Libya	531	Libya	613	Costa Rica	596
Cameroon	516	Portugal	609	Italy	594
Morocco	502	Abu Dhabi	598	Syria	558
France	454	Singapore	562	France	545
Mozambique	452	Thailand	547	Mozambique	527

1973		1974*		1975	
Australia	3,139	Australia	2,400	Iran	3,860
Iran	2,887	Iran	2,256	Australia	3,049
S. Africa	1,763	S. Africa	2,164	S. Africa	2,696
Nigeria	1,501	Turkey	1,234	Iraq	2,161
USA	1,246	Nigeria	1,003	Nigeria	1,816
Turkey	957	Zaire	896	Belgium	1,544
Switzerland	925	Italy	866	United Arab	
Libya	912	Zambia	849	Emirates	1,449
Tanzania	871	Libya	839	Zambia	1,340
Malaysia	785	Switzerland	825	Malaysia	1,303
Zambia	772	Tanzania	818	France	1,214
Angola	708	Belgium/Lux	788	Libya	1,207
France	680	France	780	Muscat & Oman	1,191
Mozambique	668	Kenya	725	Kenya	1,131
Kenya	648	Dubai	690	Zaire	1,005
New Zealand	633	Mozambique	601	Italy	635
Costa Rica	609	Norway	594	Syria	616
Thailand	602	Malaysia	577	Algeria	596
Algeria	572	Muscat & Oman	555	Turkey	530
Muscat & Oman	548	Lebanon	504	Morocco	484
				Sudan	471

*The Land-Rover was withdrawn from the United States market during 1974, because of the very high potential cost of tooling to meet North American safety and exhaust emission regulations.

1976		1977	
Iran	4,857	Iran	3,152
S. Africa	3,003	Nigeria	1,920
Nigeria	2,369	Australia	1,820
Libya	2,187	France	1,750
Australia	2,137	S. Africa	1,698
United Arab		Switzerland	1,639
Emirates	1,861	Libya	1,606
Morocco	1,428	Saudi Arabia	1,490
Sudan	1,384	Kenya	1,319
French West		Algeria	1,121
Africa	1,300	Holland	1,121
Muscat & Oman	913	United Arab	
Saudi Arabia	805	Emirates	1,069
Italy	680	Tanzania	1,010
France	678	Morocco	973
Malaysia	542	Belgium	669
Zambia	538	Malaysia	619
Belgium	489	Costa Rica	539
New Zealand	456	Muscat & Oman	536
Ethiopia	437	Indonesia	520
Costa Rica	420	West Germany	482
Indonesia	408		

4 Performance and Fuel Consumption — the Facts

Land-Rovers

	Series I 86in WB 7-seat station wagon 1,997cc petrol Autocar test, 4/3/55	Series I 107in WB 10-seat station wagon 1,997cc petrol Motor test, 18/7/56	Series IIA 88in WB pick-up 2,286cc petrol Autocar test, 19/11/65	Series IIA 109in WB 12-seat station wagon 2,625cc petrol Autocar test, 13/7/67	Series III 109in WB truck cab 2,625cc petrol Autocar test, 28/10/71
Maximum speed (mph)	58	58	67	73	69
Acceleration through gears (secs)					
0–30mph	7.1	7.8	6.9	5.8	6.6
0–40mph	—	14.7	12.3	11.3	11.3
0–50mph	25.5	28.9	19.9	17.1	17.0
0–60mph	—	—	36.1	29.0	31.7
0–70mph	—	—	—	—	—
0–80mph	—	—	—	—	—
0–90mph	—	—	—	—	—
Standing start – $\frac{1}{4}$-mile (secs)	25.7	26.2	24.0	23.6	22.9
Top gear acceleration (secs)					
10–30mph	11.4	12.7	10.2	11.3	11.9
20–40mph	12.6	15.7	13.8	13.1	12.1
30–50mph	18.2	24.7	18.2	15.8	14.4
40–60mph	—	—	22.8	19.5	24.5
50–70mph	—	—	—	—	—
60–80mph	—	—	—	—	—
70–90mph	—	—	—	—	—
Fuel consumption (mpg)					
overall recorded	21.0	18.2	18.3	13.8	14.9
typical (all conditions)	24	21	20	15	15
Weight (lb)	2,968	3,444	3,010	3,948	3,582

	Land-Rover Ninety V8 County Station Wagon	Range Rovers				
	3,528cc 5-speed Autocar test, 8/5/85	vee-8 3,528cc petrol Autocar test, 12/11/70	vee-8 3,528cc petrol Motor test, 16/1/71	vee-8 3,528cc petrol with o/d Autocar test, 1/7/78	vee-8 3,528cc petrol 5-speed Autocar test, 24/12/83	vee-8 3,528cc petrol 5-speed Autocar test, 22/10/86
Maximum speed (mph)	n.a.	91	99	96*	96	105
Acceleration through gears (secs)						
0–30mph	4.0	4.3	4.2	4.1	3.8	3.6
0–40mph	6.4	6.3	6.2	6.9	6.3	5.7
0–50mph	10.0	10.0	9.3	10.1	9.7	8.2
0–60mph	14.7	13.9	12.9	14.3	14.4	11.9
0–70mph	21.5	18.6	17.7	20.5	20.8	16.0
0–80mph	36.0	28.1	25.6	29.3	32.1	22.8
0–90mph	—	42.4	36.6	—	19.2	31.1
Standing start – ¼-mile (secs)	19.5	19.1	18.7	19.7	19.5	18.4
Top gear acceleration (secs)						
10–30mph	—	10.2	—	13.1	—	17.5
20–40mph	15.3	9.1	9.1	12.8	15.9	15.9
30–50mph	15.3	9.6	9.1	12.2	15.2	15.7
40–60mph	17.3	9.8	9.4	12.7	16.3	16.4
50–70mph	21.4	10.6	10.6	14.3	18.1	17.4
60–80mph	36.6	14.2	13.6	17.8	—	20.0
70–90mph	—	24.4	20.2	—	—	28.1
Fuel consumption (mpg)						
overall recorded	13.2	14.4	14.8	14.2	15.4	15.0
typical (all conditions)	15	16	18	15.5	17	16.5
Weight (lb)	n.a.	3,880	3,864	4,009	4,249	4,334

*In direct top, 91mph in overdrive top.

Index